FOR FIDELITY

FOR
FIDELITY

*How Intimacy and Commitment
Enrich Our Lives*

CATHERINE M. WALLACE

ALFRED A. KNOPF   NEW YORK

1998

THIS IS A BORZOI BOOK
PUBLISHED BY ALFRED A. KNOPF, INC.

Copyright © 1998 by Catherine M. Wallace
All rights reserved under International and Pan-American Copyright
Conventions. Published in the United States by Alfred A. Knopf, Inc.,
New York, and simultaneously in Canada by Random House
of Canada Limited, Toronto.
Distributed by Random House, Inc., New York.
http://www.randomhouse.com/

Some portions of this work were originally published by
Forward Movement Publications, Cincinnati, Ohio, as the
following two pamphlets: "A Sexual Ethic for My Children"
and "Relationship as Blessing."

Owing to limitations of space, all acknowledgments for
permission to reprint previously published material may
be found following the Index.

Library of Congress Cataloging-in-Publication Data
Wallace, Catherine Miles.
For fidelity : how intimacy and commitment enrich our lives /
by Catherine M. Wallace.—1st ed.
p.   cm.
Includes bibliographical references and index.
ISBN 0-375-40079-6 (hc).—ISBN 0-375-70072-2 (tp)
1. Sex—Religious aspects—Christianity.
2. Commitment (Psychology)—Religious aspects—Christianity.
3. Sex instruction for children—Religious aspects—Christianity.
4. Sexual ethics.
1. Title
BT708.W34   1998
241'.66—dc21   97-36677
CIP

Manufactured in the United States of America
First Edition

To Warren H. Wallace, M.D.

Let me not to the marriage of true minds
Admit impediments. Love is not love
Which alters when it alteration finds
Or bends with the remover to remove.
O, no! it is an ever-fixèd mark,
That looks on tempests and is never shaken;
It is the star to every wandering bark,
Whose worth's unknown, although his height be taken.
Love's not Time's fool, though rosy lips and cheeks
Within his bending sickle's compass come;
Love alters not with his brief hours and weeks,
But bears it out even to the edge of doom.
    If this be error, and upon me proved,
    I never writ, nor no man ever loved.

—William Shakespeare, Sonnet 116

For one thing, sires, safely dare I say,
That friends each other must obey,
If they will long hold company.
Love will not be constrained by mastery.
When mastery comes, the God of Love quick
Beats his wings, and farewell, he is gone!
Love is a thing as any spirit free. . . .
Look who that is most patient in love,
He is at an advantage all above.
Patience is a high virtue, certainly,
For it vanquishes, as these scholars say,
Things that rigor will never attain.

—Geoffrey Chaucer, *The Canterbury Tales*

Contents

Preface

This book began in honest perplexity, where most good books begin: How do some people remain happily married and faithful to each other? That question quickly led to a bigger one. How is it that trust and honor have become daringly countercultural? An independent local merchant declines my offer of identification when I write a check, looking me in the eye with something close to proud and angry defiance. I return an excess $10 bill given me in change by a clerk. She eyes me cautiously, knowingly: *Oh, it's one of* those *people.* Bumper stickers advocate kindness as a subversive, liberating "random act"—not as a habitual practice.

Another title for this book might be "the plight of troth," a lovely old phrase that can mean both "the predicament of trust" and "the promise of fidelity." I keep to my specific topic, sexual fidelity in long-term, committed relationships, but the bigger questions cast shadows I cannot avoid. What is fidelity between people? What do we promise when we promise to be faithful? How does fidelity work? Why does it matter? On the other hand, why is it so hard? And why, in our day, do we seem as a society to be losing the capacity both for trust and for trustworthiness? I am also interested in how we teach kids, but that too is the local form of a bigger question about the nurture and transmission of moral tradition.

My perspective on these larger issues is determined by what I can glimpse of the Wisdom that calls us to be compassionate and not merely competitive, to serve and not merely to succeed. Ancient voices insist that there is more to life than earning a living and greater depths within us than individualist self-actualizing can plumb. The deep and abiding human passions are a sacred fire in the heart: We need in every age to find new ways to gather around that circle.

My specific and most important presuppositions have been articulated best by poets. John Keats, for instance: "I am certain of nothing but the holiness of the heart's affections and the truth of imagination."[1] William Blake: "Prudence is a rich ugly old maid courted by Incapacity," and "Exuberance is Beauty."[2] William Shakespeare: "Let me not to the marriage of true minds / Admit impediments. Love is not love / Which alters when it alteration finds."[3] My argument also derives from my scholarly work many years ago on Samuel Taylor Coleridge and his theory of imagination. Coleridge was both poet and theologian. He was absolutely convinced that spiritual realities permeate every aspect of experience and weave themselves into every line of inquiry, no matter how rigorously abstract or apparently remote. As Blake cautions, infinity can fit in the palm of your hand, eternity in an hour.[4] It's an odd way to get through the day, if you take this idea seriously. And I do. And so I am convinced that faithful, absolutely committed marriage is the creative work of imagination.

This book is also grounded in a visionary and Coleridgean reading of Christianity. I realize that many Christians—and some Coleridgeans as well—will be deeply offended by that claim. Many others, I hope, will not. Explicitly theological issues are confined to notes, where the curious or the angry can locate at least a little of the modern scholarship delineating how Christianity itself is or can be a profoundly wise and deeply imaginative Western engagement with the human experience of the Holy. But I am a literary critic, not a professionally trained theologian. I trespass. Nonetheless, poets and priests were once the same people, and truth carried alive into the heart by passion remains a central human need no matter how subspecialized our graduate schools.

I want to express my thanks for a wholly fortuitous set of speaking and publication opportunities offered to me by various parishes and organizations within the Episcopal church. Charles Long, Robert Horine, and Edward Stone Gleason at Forward Movement Publications in Cincinnati have published and held in print several of these talks, produced as those little tracts found on racks in the vestibules of churches. Robert Horine in particular kept nudging me to write a book. I am pleased to acknowledge the permission of Forward Movement to repeat parts of arguments first published by them.

On the basis of the first tract, "A Sexual Ethic for My Children," Mark Waldo and the Diocese of Virginia invited me to the Blue Ridge Mountains to address the annual Family Conference. At the end of that week, a group of grandmothers presented a hilarious song-and-dance routine summarizing and brilliantly critiquing my entire argument. It was a well-rhymed display of the shrewd wit for which Southern women are famous. But the "Glory Sisters" also delineated for me crucial connections among the scattered parts of my presentations. Writers dream of such thorough engagement with a work in progress as the Family Conference community offered me that summer. Of course, Anglicans have always been noted for their sympathy with literary people. But they are equally famous for each keeping his or her own counsel, especially in difficult and controversial matters. And that's exactly what has made them such a wonderful audience.

I have also been blessed, far beyond rhyme or reason, by friends who have shared my perplexity, talked openly about their youth and their marriages, laughed at my stories, urged me to write, and facilitated all of these wonderful public opportunities. The couple of weeks after Knopf called were one unending celebration in my little corner of the world. Although I have made changes to protect the privacy of my friends, I've used so many of their stories that I cannot name them in public now without risk of betraying a trust. I know their names are written in gold, gold to airy thinness beat, in some finer pages than these.

Thanks are also due to my friends at Northminster Presbyterian Church, including Anne Fisher, interim senior pastor, Steven Durham, associate pastor, and Catherine Sarkesian, director of religious education. My arguments about narrative and about storytelling as a spiritual resource were first presented as a series of parish talks; a second series of talks on sexual ethics prompted invaluable clarifications of my thinking on several key points. The Presbyterians are at times a bit bewildered to find a "literalist of the imagination" in their midst, incessantly looking around for "imaginary gardens with real toads in them."[5] I in turn cannot fathom Calvin's God. But I am pleased to acknowledge how much I have been blessed by sharp questions and warm hospitality.

I am pleased also to acknowledge the kindness and the friendship of Stanley Hauerwas. I send him poetry; he sends me theology; we argue about the politics and the poetics of God-talk. It has been a fruitful and challenging correspondence for me, in no small measure because he also argues that I must stop pitching my tent in the margins and instead make a faithful commitment to a specific congregation. He has not yet made a proper theologian of me, nor I a poet of him—but the arguments are still under way. I owe more to his thinking and his bibliographic suggestions than my notes alone reveal.

Warm thanks are also due to Timothy Sedgwick, a friend and one-time neighbor with whom I have argued both Coleridgean sacramental theology and the metaphoric substructures of Christian asceticism. Tim introduced me to his friend Jane Garrett at Knopf; she has been both kind and generous. (My kids have taken to calling her "Saint Jane.") Robert Olsson designed a text whose voice matches mine with uncanny precision. Karen Deaver, production editor, and Connie Oehring, freelance copy editor, corrected mistakes both egregious and subtle with an unfailing courteous restraint that, having been an editor myself, I know to be the labor of love. Claire Bradley Ong, production manager, has kept my head spinning in the effort to keep up with her quick and well-organized process. Writing per se is lonely work, and such fine company has been delightful.

Finally, my three adolescent children are not fictional characters although they would, I suspect, prefer to disavow the tales I tell about them: It has to be tough on a teenager for Mom to be out in public talking and writing about sex. Their resilience has been remarkable and their support mature and kindly. My husband is bemused but generous: He married me, he says, when he was young and foolish. That's an excuse. The truth is that he has always insisted that I simply have to have a room of my own, even when he had to take a week's vacation to build partitions and shelves and wire outlets for me. After I decided to stay home full-time with the children, he provided the economic, practical, and emotional support I needed to read and to write without concern for paying the mortgage or accounting to anyone. His fidelity, in the deepest, richest sense of that word, underlies this book.

. . .

The organization of what follows is as straightforward as I can make it. The topic is sexual relationships, so Chapter Two is on sexual desire and Chapter Three is on intimate relationships. The question at hand about sexual relationships is, When they are good, what's so good about them? That's Chapter Four, which takes a close look at some familiar Bible stories defining a quality I call "blessing." I conclude each chapter with some suggestions about how parents may encourage the moral development of their children in these regards; I draw that line of thought to its conclusion in Chapter Five. After I did all this, I went back and revised Chapter One so as to lay before you my principal conclusion: Sexual fidelity is crucial to achieving the best that our own sexuality can offer to each of us.

FOR FIDELITY

CHAPTER ONE

Accounting for Fidelity

Facing Questions in the Dark

"Does Daddy use condoms?"

I stopped grinding coffee beans and looked across the dark, November-morning kitchen at my eight-year-old son, who had set aside his raisin toast with peanut butter. The kitchen smelled of cinnamon and peanuts and coffee.

"Mark says—Mark says the teacher says if you don't use condoms then you could both get sick and die. So we want to know. Does he? Every time?"

I looked down from that level, blue-eyed gaze, wishing I could eat coffee beans like peanuts, straight from the little bag. Apparently Mark had been talking to his brother about his fifth-grade "sex ed" course, sharing his fears about orphanages in their endless brotherly small talk after lights out. When a kid has totally uncool parents, when his parents were probably nerds when they were kids, a kid needs to ask these questions. A kid can't count on parents like that to know the important stuff—not even when Daddy is a professor in the medical school downtown.

When I had sex ed, we didn't worry about our parents dying. One afternoon in 1964, the eighth graders gathered in the parish auditorium to listen to the curate explain about sperm and fallopian tubes and why girls should sit with their knees together. (The three nuns listening from the side nodded approvingly at this last point; I was watching them. They taught us everything else. Why bring in the curate for this? Maybe nuns didn't know about fallopian tubes.) Then we marched, single file and in silence, back to our crowded classrooms.

Fallopian tubes and sin, I wondered to myself. Surely there is more to sex than this. Don't nuns and priests ever go to James Bond movies?

Probably not, I realized.

Sex education, 1990s style, is fallopian tubes and death. Sex and death. Not "death," that favorite synonym for orgasm in the love-sonnet tradition. No, sex and Pneumocystis carinii pneumonia and viral encephalitis and Kaposi's sarcoma. Sex and AIDS, like sex and sin, is supposed to help him "just say no." But surely there are greater truths about sexuality that the grownups are still not telling the kids.

So I set aside the coffee grinder and struggled to find the right words to reassure my son. As his tears brimmed and splashed down onto the peanut butter, I heard myself talking about my marriage as if it were based primarily on sexual exclusivity, as if my own sexual behavior were grounded primarily in nothing more than property rights and the fear of contagion. But what would that fear be worth when this gutsy and forthright kid discovered his own mature sexuality? The threat of eternal damnation hadn't stopped me, not for a minute. And what's a mere virus in comparison with hell? I knew I had to do better than that. I had to do better for them, for Tim and Carol, who are twins, and for Mark, our firstborn. I felt that I owed them a more accurate and intelligible account of anything so important in my life and in theirs as this marriage.

But I had to do better for myself too. Why are my husband and I faithful to each other sexually? I knew that our sexual exclusivity is not simply obedience to the prohibitions handed down to us once upon a time. Like many other baby boomers, we had simply dismissed as nonsense the whole hierarchical structure of repression, exclusion, and exploitation within which those rules were traditionally enshrined. But since the '60s, some new understanding of, some new commitment to sexual fidelity had obviously grown up in its place. I didn't know what it was, and I didn't know how to account for it over breakfast except in the negative and utilitarian terms of property rights and public health.

I think that my predicament is widely shared. Having attained a certain age, we have in one way or another come to terms with our own sexual needs. We have made the various decisions about sexuality that life demands of us, and we cope with the consequences as gracefully as we can. But from what I can tell, talking to people here and there, most of us did so pragmatically, ad hoc, here and now, in this situation with this partner, not because we had worked through the issues in thoughtful and thorough ways. Our world, our times, did not permit such working through, at least not in much of this nation.

Nonetheless, many of us have muddled our way into middle age on the whole quite successfully. If we are now settled into faithful relationships, if we now treasure what we have and hope our kids do as well for themselves, we have gotten to this point through a bewildering mix of conscious motives, unconscious internalization, and what often feels like lucky breaks and arbitrary choices. We have trouble accounting—even to ourselves—for the choices that have shaped our lives. My presentations in parish settings have strongly convinced me that this difficulty is as much the case for ordinary churchgoers as for anyone else: In our sexual lives or as sexual couples, we have and we cherish something that inherited religious traditions have trouble articulating plainly and directly except in the bloodless legal language of mandated exclusivity. Even believers tend not, these days, to pay much attention to church authority as such. (I now make my bed in the morning too—not because my mother once made me but because it's my only hope for my half of the covers the next night.) Whether we are churchgoers or whether we sit home in our pajamas reading the newspaper, I suggest, very many in our generation have decided to cope with our sexual needs in our own ways and on our own terms, whether or not we can articulate those terms to ourselves or to our teenagers.

No matter what, we can't say to our kids, "Just say no." That's simply not an option for most of our generation. We came of age when "tradition" and "authority" were derogatory terms, when the whole post-Enlightenment worldview, shattered left and right by Stalin and by Hitler, was being swept offstage altogether. I was eighteen and living in Chicago when the police rioted during the 1968 Democratic Convention. I was exactly the age of several of the students who died at Kent State—while the brother nearest to me in age was switched from his usual task of flying body bags out to the Philippines and sent to bomb Cambodia. These are the images of "traditional authority" that were seared into my soul.

Now the scars are no longer so livid. Now we ourselves wield much of the power against which we once rebelled. But unanswered questions still lurk in the shadows, and sexual fidelity is among them. We questioned traditional sexual arrangements just as powerfully as we questioned traditional political arrangements. But now we have kids who face the reality of AIDS: Premarital abstinence sounds better and better as the months tick past. Or we have nightmares about paying both for childcare and for college if the unwanted pregnancy of a dependent teenager renders us grandparents (*grandparents?*) before our time.

Most powerfully of all, we have learned a lot that we once could not imagine. We have reaped the blessings that follow from sexual fidelity; we have discovered the comfort and the strength that committed relationships engender, even though plenty of us have gone through divorces and remarried. We have grown up since the days when we were immortal, omnipotent, omniscient, and skinny. And sexy. And unwilling to trust anyone *over* thirty. We have earned our own small share in the world's deep and ancient wisdom, a precious heritage we hope somehow to transmit.

I was startled to realize how tough it can be to find ways to explain all this to our kids. If anyone ought to know what to say, I thought to myself angrily, it's someone like me, with the kind of education I have had. But I didn't. And everyone I knew well enough to ask faced the prospect of these teen years with the same dread and uncertainty that my husband and I were feeling.

Nor was it clear, at first, where to look for help. It seems to me that the mainline Protestant denominations are discovering the sexual revolution just as everyone else discovers fatal sexually transmitted diseases and starts looking around for some better and clearer understanding of fidelity, some nonrepressive, nonpunitive argument for abstinence. They are debating the humanity of homosexuals with all the bizarre seriousness with which the ancient world wondered whether women have souls or the early-modern world evaluated the humanity of people of color. The Roman Catholic Church maintains its prohibition of birth control, although plenty of American Catholics—supported by compassionate clergy—quietly ignore the Pope. But the Vatican expends tremendous resources to enforce the ban elsewhere in the world and to silence even responsible scholarly debate of the issues. The silencing of debate blurs the crucial distinction between moral authority and simple authoritarianism.

Furthermore, both Protestant and Catholic accounts deduce sexual morals from a complex array of abstract, densely encoded theological propositions about the nature of God, the authority of tradition, and the character of the Bible. I am not persuaded. I am a believer—albeit on the margins[1]—but that is not *how* I believe. Sexual fidelity is for me not an intellectual stance but an intensely embodied practice. It is a high-energy, habitual approach to my physical life as a red-blooded woman who is sexually attracted to men. It is not an idea, not a conclusion deduced from premises.

Sexual fidelity is not an idea for any of us, I suspect, churched and unchurched alike. Plenty of us are faithful to our spouses and opposed to casual sex by our kids, whether or not we have studied theology or pledged allegiance to a church. Our reasons are articulated neither by the abstruse arguments of theologians nor by the narrow self-interest calculations of social scientists. Nor, for those of us who schlepp out on the Sabbath, do sermons say why. Preachers explicate elaborate doctrines and ancient texts. Conservatives may advocate obedience to authority; liberals may advocate soup kitchens in the city or social justice in Central America. But parish clergy in general seem to me quite reluctant to trespass upon the sacred ground of "private" matters. It is much safer to explain the arcane than to address the very tough moral choices we face in our everyday lives both at work and at home.

"Make up your own minds," we are told. And that's what
our kids are taught in sex ed. And so we are left standing in
dark kitchens, wondering what to say about why we live as
we do, facing these solemn-eyed kids.

I am not professionally trained in Christian theology,
although I am theologically literate. I can more or less hold
my own regarding the philosophic array of fundamental
questions and answers on either side of the Reformation.
That literacy doesn't help. Even if it did, I can't use theological razzle-dazzle on my own kids: They don't go to church.
Our experience with local congregations has been painful at
times, and the kids have become even more wary than I am.
Under any circumstances, I doubt that church authority as
such would influence their sexual behavior. My husband and
I have always encouraged them to think critically. It's much
too late for anyone to try pontificating on something as complicated and contentious as sexual behavior. Their questions
are sharp and skeptical. They expect good answers that I have
struggled to find.

We all need answers for our kids, answers that are honest
and useful and sensitive. Consider this: All of us help our
kids with homework. We guide them carefully through the
selection of classes for next year. We discuss what warrant
the orthodontist has for insisting on floss or on retainers, and
we laugh together at Joe Camel ads. We facilitate relationships with teachers and coaches; we mediate the power of
peer pressure. We put apples and carrots in their lunches
every day, and we struggle to keep pepperoni pizza to whatever minimal level adolescent metabolism actively demands.
We help them plan parties and respond appropriately to a
considerable array of social situations created by the many
varieties of blended families and—at least where we live—by
the dazzling diversity of a multicultural community. In

short, we give them a lot of intelligent help in every domain
of their lives. They have always counted on us, and we have
always done our best to provide. Adolescence is not a good
time to abandon them to their own "opinions."

I remember the day one of mine (who pleads to remain
nameless) calmly announced a decision to stop bathing
because showers were boring. We are wise to respect our
kids' opinions and choices, but only up to a certain point.
For ourselves as well as for them, we make crucial distinctions when theory comes to practice, when postmodern push
comes to shove. To do otherwise is deeply irresponsible. For
instance, I have read enough about particle physics to understand that the brick wall of the house is not as solid as it
seems but rather is seething and indeterminate. Nonetheless,
it would leave quite a dent: I back the car down the driveway
very carefully indeed. No theory, no matter how elaborate
and persuasive, can soften a brick wall. And life is full of
brick walls, in morals as in real estate: Postmodern skepticism reaches its horizon when an eight-year-old confronts
you about safe sex. We have to talk to our kids, no matter
how many gray hairs it earns us.

One way or another, consciously and deliberately or who
knows how, we are already advising them on their sexuality.
There is no way not to, because sexual ethics is a variety or a
species of interpersonal ethics, and their crucial model for
interpersonal relationships is their relationship with us.
When we tried to teach our toddlers to say please, to take
turns, to share, not to hit, we were only making explicit what
we had already taught by example. We were teaching them
how to be friends, which is a very complex course of study.
Sexual relationships are the most highly charged of friendships, the highest-stakes relationships most of us will ever
know. The friendships that are our marriages are—for better

and for worse—our kids' crucial model as well. But once again, it's up to us to make that model explicit and, en route, once again to do as much as we can to enunciate ideals that our own lives can only partially illustrate.

As parents of teenagers or almost-teens, our only real choice is how conscious to be of what we are doing, how consistent, how systematic, and above all how comfortable with ourselves in discussing the erotic as such. And that's where this book comes in. Real consistency, real clarity, demands the kind of thoughtful understanding of the erotic that most of us never achieved as young adults. We need now to account to our kids for our own mature engagement with sexuality, to account for what time has taught us—the hard way, at times—about sexually active relationships. This book is my best effort to think through these issues in a way that I hope you will find intellectually responsible and ethically focused but neither authoritarian nor doctrinaire. But this is not a how-to book, not a later version of *Toilet Training in Less Than a Day*. *How* has to be happenstance. *How* will happen only in response to their questions and to their little sleight-of-hand comments.

We also need to think through the issues for our own sakes, because the sexual transition that is their adolescence is a transition for us too. The sexual maturity of one's offspring is a disconcerting encounter with one's own aging. The tumult between parents and teens is clearly stirred up from both sides, because the temptation to deny their growing up is deeply seated in all of us. Sex and death, after all, have always been elaborately intertwined concepts in our culture. Among the richest fruits of our own maturity, as I see it, is the ability to face our children's sexual development with some measure of equanimity precisely because whatever we once had of sexy, youthful allure has developed into that richer, deeper sense of self that can look upon gray hair through bifocals and be unshaken. It's tough. We have to be able to laugh together, and to laugh at ourselves, or we will indeed succumb to that ancient curse: Just Wait 'til You Have Children of Your Own.

It has taken me several years and several very generous audiences to elaborate the argument I will be presenting: That bright-eyed third-grader is now in high school. Last time we checked, he stood six inches taller than I—and even that is changing fast. Amidst the reality of my life with three teenagers, my need to define an intelligible sexual ethics has never been a theoretical project or an academic undertaking. I have done my best to situate major issues within historical and cultural contexts so we can help our kids "map" or "locate" the various claims about sexuality that they hear. They are being taught to do that in all their social-sciences courses, after all: It's fun, and it's tremendously useful. But I am not concerned with history as such. I have endeavored in every way to write a pragmatic book, a direct and down-to-earth book for those of us who stand in kitchens on dark mornings wondering about the decisions that so deeply inform whatever meaning our lives have. I have not endeavored to write a book you can hand to your teenagers instead of listening to them, but I have worked long and hard to craft explanations that you can steal easily and with confidence and quickly adapt to your own circumstances and particular priorities.

Fidelity as Moral Norm

In the chapters that follow, I will make the best, the most direct, the most unabashed argument I know how to make on behalf of the traditional virtue usually called "sexual fidelity" or "monogamy," a virtue that calls casual sex into question even among the unmarried. Sexual fidelity is more than sexual exclusivity. Sexual exclusivity is a negative, minimalist, and merely proscriptive concept. It defines a certain quality of physical and psychic property rights, but nothing more. Yet there is something more to marriage—or there can be something more, as some of us have slowly realized. Neither "sexual fidelity" nor "monogamy" perfectly names what I'm getting at, but these are the names we have. For the rest of this chapter, I want to delineate some of the boundaries of my definition of this "something more."

When I say I will argue directly for fidelity, I mean I will explicate and defend sexual fidelity for its own sake and not on behalf of other good things that follow from it or from which it follows. For instance, I will not argue for its utility in preventing venereal disease, or insuring the financial support and authenticity of one's offspring, or sustaining a social order dependent upon coherent family structures. Nor will I argue that fidelity follows from the concept of justice, or the marriage contract, or any of the modern versions of ancient property rights. Nor will I argue that sexual fidelity is commanded by God's demand: "Thou shalt not commit adultery."

I have no particular objection to any of these arguments, of course. Some of them are quite important. But none offers what seems to me a sufficient account of sexuality fidelity, because in all of them sexual fidelity is something extrinsic to the marital relationship itself. Monogamy is simply the means to some good and useful end outside itself, whether avoiding a virus or avoiding damnation or avoiding social chaos. I will argue instead that sexual fidelity is a practice *intrinsic* to the happiness of a happy marriage.

Before we go any further, however, let me answer a question that I suppose is on every reader's mind by this point.

What about gays and lesbians? Specifically, what about gays or lesbians, sexual fidelity, and marriage? Do I use the term "marriage" in some exclusive sense? No. I'll have a little more to say about the terminology of relationships later on, when we need it, but for now the simple direct reply is sufficient. If your kid turns out to be gay, or your kid's best friend, does that mean none of this argument applies to them? Do you give your kid permission to be promiscuous? Is your kid suddenly somehow incapable of integrity? Do you demand absolute abstinence forever and ever, amen? Do you turn the kid out of the house as depraved and a scandal to the family? I can't imagine any of that. Those who claim basis in the Gospel for such brutal behavior are not reading those books with adequate historical, cultural, and sociological discipline.[2] Nor are they attending to Jesus' own inclusive and compassionate regard for the marginalized, especially those marginalized by notions of spiritual impurity.[3]

The anger directed at gays and lesbians frightens me, so I might avoid the issue altogether if I could. But that's not possible. I have discovered that I cannot account adequately for my own sexuality while excluding theirs. So at various points I will stop and repeat that all of this argument applies to all of us equally. But in fact I am writing primarily as a parent to other parents, so I will inevitably refer most often to the shared experiences of husbands and wives. My "position" concerning homosexuality—since it seems I have to have one—is that I reject the grounds on which sexual orientation is defined as a moral question in the first place.

Furthermore, I have some sympathy for the complaint that gays and lesbians are more than a little weary of being stared at and talked about by the rest of us. In Japan I attracted some staring and global disapproval because I am left-handed; I hadn't felt that much attention to the matter since learning to print in kindergarten, when the other kids at my table were distraught (so was I, in short order). The staring felt rude, and it felt presumptuous.

Fidelity as Intrinsic to Marriage

I have said that sexual fidelity is intrinsic to the happiness of a good marriage. What do I mean by "intrinsic"? I take the concept from Alasdair MacIntyre, for whom it is central to an elegant argument about the character of virtue and about how virtue is transmitted from one generation to the next.[4] With some apology to Professor MacIntyre, however, I want to suggest that "intrinsic" can best be understood—at least for our purposes—by thinking about cinnamon rolls. As it happens, I am very fond of cinnamon rolls.

The ordinary cinnamon roll has a rich yeast bread as its basis: After the dough rises, you punch it down, roll it out, sprinkle around a more or less scandalous quantity of butter and brown sugar and spices, roll it up into a log, slice the log into pinwheels, let the pinwheels rise a second time, and then bake. It takes almost forever because the eggs and the butter in the dough slow the rising. That's why I usually go to the Great Harvest bakery over on Central Street, though I tell myself it's because theirs are whole-wheat. (A Jesuit education ought never to be slighted.)

But I have discovered that something quite passable can be had by substituting biscuit dough for yeast dough. The advantage of biscuit dough is that you don't have to wait hours for the dough to rise. Biscuits are made with baking powder, not yeast. If you are skilled at the rolling and slicing, the whole thing takes about half an hour, plus twenty minutes to bake.

The only problem with these biscuit-dough cinnamon things is that their texture is all wrong. Real cinnamon rolls, made properly with yeast, have a slightly chewy texture because the yeast interacts with the warm milk and the wheat protein in complex ways. Baking powder doesn't do that. In fact, the best biscuits are made with low-protein flour so as to produce something that is flaky and tender rather than chewy.

In short, yeast is *intrinsic* to the bread dough from which cinnamon rolls are properly made. My cinnamon biscuits are tasty, of course—they are wolfed down in minutes around here—but they are not real cinnamon rolls because they are biscuits, not rolls. Rolls require yeast.

Marriage requires sexual fidelity in the same way. Like yeast, fidelity is a growing, living thing that interacts with and transforms and reorganizes all the other ingredients of the relationship. There's no other way to concoct what I understand as a marriage. Other sorts of relationships have their merits, just as my cinnamon biscuits or my chocolate-chip cookies do. But my interest here is in understanding how to "make" what I have come to recognize as marriage. There is no marriage without sexual fidelity, just as there is no cinnamon roll without yeast. You might as well try leaving out the cinnamon.

A good marriage, a happy and rewarding and self-sustaining one, is a work of art. And in saying that, I mean to insist that I cannot hope to give you directions as consistently reliable as my recipe for cinnamon rolls. If you can read and measure accurately, you can make these utterly splendid cinnamon rolls whenever you have a free afternoon. There is nothing elusive about this kind of plain, everyday cooking. Of course, a recent issue of *Bon Appetit* tried to make an art out of fixing macaroni and cheese, but the melodrama of that effort just proves my point. Many good things in life are simple, straightforward, and under control, but a really happy marriage is not one of them. There is something powerfully elusive about any art, including the art of a happy marriage.

I don't mean to say that marriage is magic or that we can gloss our way through the issues raised by fidelity with some soft-focus sentimentality. I cannot give you a recipe for writing a great poem, but as a literary critic with a Ph.D. in English I can certainly explain a lot about how poems succeed or fail as poems. The success of a good poem or a good painting or a good movie is also neither magic nor simply good luck. The success of an art cannot be fully described in the logical and mechanical terms of engineering blueprints because creativity is not a matter of logic and mechanics and the calculations of stress. Yet between magic and mechanics there is a vast domain of human experience wherein we inherit genuinely important wisdom about how to live our lives. And that domain is where we are headed.

Sexual Fidelity as Artistic Discipline

Before we head that way, however, I want to sketch three implications of the idea that fidelity is intrinsic to marriage. The first is that fidelity does not produce happiness in the way that a factory produces widgets. It's not quid pro quo in that way, this for that, trade a little fidelity for a little happiness or a lot of fidelity for riotous delight morning after morning for happily ever after. Life is not that simple. Those who are faithful enjoy something that those who are not faithful do not enjoy, but fidelity is not a means to the end of joy in the way that a light switch is a means to turning on a light.

Instead, marriage is much more like playing the flute. Listening to a James Galway recording one afternoon, I was stunned by a complex passage that Galway played with deep and delicate passion. He made the music sound effortless, the feelings seem utterly lucid, as if playing the flute were as simple as breathing and our feelings were as plain as the fingers on our hands. And then the passage kept going and kept going without pause for breath until I was almost convinced that the recording would end when the poor man passed out cold and crashed to the floor from lack of air. How did he do it? How could anyone do it?

As I got up to replay the recording, I had a sudden vision of just how many lonely hours of practice must lie behind such a performance. How many hours alone in a room, playing and listening and playing again, how much study, how much a whole life centered on music and on this particular instrument? These few moments of surpassing beauty were the fruit of such a life, the gift that proves, as Shelley puts it, that silence and solitude are not vacancy, that the incessant solitude of a man alone with his art is a solitude nonetheless deeply shared and powerfully human.[5]

The paradox here is that the glorious performance does not "repay" such hours. Even for those with world-class talent, the glory of a splendid performance or the financial rewards of commercial success do not measure up against the time and effort expended, in part because the expenditure is far too great and in part—in larger part—because the governing reality here is not quid pro quo, this for that, these hours in a practice room for that glorious recording or that thunderous applause following live performance. Galway practices his flute because he is a flutist. That is his life. It is his calling to be a particular kind of person with a particular kind of life. It is what once was called a "discipline," which is to say a defining or characteristic set of choices, virtues, and activities. Listening to Wynton Marsalis, to Itzhak Perlman, one can hear the depths of experience that such discipline allows them to articulate for the rest of us.

And so with marriage. Sexual fidelity cannot guarantee marital happiness, just as practicing the flute cannot guarantee a booking at Carnegie Hall. On the other hand, no one gets such a booking who has not practiced with real devotion, with devotion that arises from some deeper and richer place than the hope for recompense. And so too, those who experience the kind of genuinely happy marriages that I'm trying to describe are those for whom the virtue of fidelity is a central discipline shaping their lives—not merely a good investment of energies.

Or to put the same idea in yet another way: I write because I am a writer, because I have been called to work at becoming a writer, and not because it is prudent or financially rewarding or even consistently fun as a process. As a process it is terribly lonely, especially for independent writers like me; as a process it tends to generate dry eyes, stiff necks, and computer-screen headaches. Nonetheless, writing is deeply part of who I am and also who I am becoming. I am a writer for the sake of writing, which is also to say for my own sake and not for what it might bring me. I would not just be miserable if I stopped writing; I would probably become someone other than who I am now.

So too, I am faithful because I am a wife, because I have committed myself to being a wife, and not because fidelity can be adequately characterized in the same terms we use to describe a good or prudent investment. I am faithful not for the sake of getting something in return but as an expression of who I have come to understand that I am, and furthermore who I ought to be, a little more clearly with each passing year. I could not be unfaithful without becoming someone else.

Such self-understanding comes very slowly to anyone. And that's the second implication of "intrinsic." The practice of the virtue, like the practice of the flute, grows and develops as a person grows and develops. It arises slowly and only with strong, persistent effort. A child may learn not to lie, but only an adult realizes—slowly and over time—the full significance of integrity in our lives. A child may learn not to hit, but it takes a lot of time and a lot of experience to begin to appreciate the true complexity of nonviolence. A younger adult—a teenager, perhaps—may learn to abstain for now from genital sexuality, but a full understanding of sexual fidelity takes decades. That full understanding arises not from abstract studies but from an embodied life: The only way to learn about integrity is to begin by not lying, as one begins to understand nonviolence by not hitting or begins to understand sexual fidelity by not having casual sex.

It is only a beginning, only a place to clear and then stand in as the first stage of an art. If I were an art teacher, I might say, "Take this blank sheet of handmade paper, but don't draw on it. First you must see it as a field, as a place infinitely rich in possibilities, and, in its own color and texture and light, as a very real thing and not as merely blank." In the same way, virginity is not a blank, a void, an absence of pleasure and of experience. It is itself a vital reality, the boundary and the domain within which a person can come to create something marvelous. But first it has to be seen clearly, which depends upon seeing and appreciating the fabulous complexity of what sexuality and sexual relationships actually entail.

My friend Bonnie is both a composer and a novelist, and as such she is a marvelous teller of tales about musicians. At Steinway Hall in New York, she says, there is a fantastic warren of little practice rooms holding enormous grand pianos and not much else. Prior to a performance, musicians can sign up for practice time rather as other folk reserve court time for racquetball or tennis. And as at the YMCA, people sometimes overstay their allotted time. One day one of Bonnie's classmates was nearly tackled by a staff person as he reached out to knock impatiently at the door of his assigned room. The staff member then opened the door himself and tiptoed inside.

The door opened again shortly thereafter. The occupant emerged, a tiny, white-haired man looking rumpled and exhausted. In heavily accented English he apologized most sincerely and, bowing slightly, held the door open for the young pianist. It was Arthur Rubinstein.

The young man sat on the bench still warm from the great maestro, quite unable at first to concentrate on his own work. When his time was up, he telephoned Bonnie and they went out for coffee. He told her what had happened. They sat together in a deli, she recalls, two thoroughly awed teenagers. Even the likes of Rubinstein, they knew, spend grinding hours alone in the lonely rooms where faithful musicians find their fidelity not only tested and rewarded but also shared by a community and by the tradition that sustains a community over time. One begins by not skipping practice, which simultaneously involves respecting the integrity of another's practice time. However well they understood that fidelity in theory, it was nonetheless stunning to witness it directly in the exhaustion and courtesy of a great artist. When Bonnie told me this story she was forty-one— torn between laughter and tears, remembering.

We come to understand the practice that is sexual fidelity in the same way, in part by our own experience and in part by the example set us by others.[6] Like the young musician, we see and we need to see that those who have gone before us, those whose example inspires us, are themselves familiar with the nitty-gritty realities of ordinary life. Marriage, like music, is not moment after moment of formal dress, spotlights, and thunderous applause. Most of life happens in something more like those little rooms in the basement of Steinway Hall, the routine reality of meals and laundry and paying the bills and taking turns in the shower in the morning. On some occasions, some people will be called upon for the equivalent of public performances of sexual fidelity. But for most of us, for most of our lives, sexual fidelity is an intimate, abiding, fundamental reality shaping the meaning of our marriages—no less crucial for being so entirely mundane, like a great maestro looking rumpled and tired.

Sexual Fidelity and Storytelling

For a little while some years ago, I belonged to a Bible-study group. One Wednesday night I told the other members that Warren and I were within days of celebrating our twentieth wedding anniversary. Across the murmur of congratulations, Christine laughed and waved her hand dismissively.

"Twenty years? Twenty years? Ha! Joe and I have more than fifty." Tiny and frail, Christine looked around the room with the grand self-possession of a matriarch, like a little black-eyed sparrow but with the regal bearing of a hawk. When she turned from the group to look at me, everyone else looked at me too.

"Kate and Warren? They're just kids, good kids, but still just getting started. Twenty years? Just wait, just wait. You'll see." She turned to Joe, and so did everyone else. Joe turned just a bit pink and looked just a bit uncomfortable. But then he smiled and shrugged and looked me in the eye and nodded, acknowledging something more than what his wife had just said. Everyone laughed very hard, and I wondered how many of them were thinking about the similarities between Joe's reserved demeanor and that of my husband. And then it was my turn to get pink and look away, flustered. But when I looked up, Christine was beaming at me.

I had been blessed. And I knew it. The congratulations of those my own age were welcome, but Christine and Joe offered a much deeper and richer affirmation. Married people do not outgrow the need for such affirmation, precisely because fidelity is *intrinsic*. What fidelity meant in my twenties is not what it will mean when I am seventy-something. I am still learning how to do this, and I still need both example and encouragement. And the complex vitality of Christine and Joe's relationship, even after half a century, testifies that their marriage is still growing and they too are still learning to live with one another. What it means to be a great master at an art is to be learning continually, just as Monet delineated so much that is central in modern abstract art both despite and because of the fact that his vision was deteriorating with age. Like Monet, Ansel Adams and Georgia O'Keeffe also reveal the ever deepening vitality and spiritual vision that can come with practice faithfully sustained over decades.

Finally, what it means that fidelity is intrinsic is that fidelity cannot be understood "in general" but only in stories. I do not live "in general" and neither do you. I live in Chicago. You live where you live. Any account of the happiness of a good marriage, the art of a good marriage, is necessarily embedded in narratives, in stories of particular lives like yours and mine, like Christine's and Joe's.[7] Plato aside, there is no such thing as Marriage. There are only particular marriages: good, bad, or indifferent; miserable or contented; growing or moribund. Marriages are real relationships between real people. Marriage is not a "state" but a spiritual journey.

Sexual fidelity, like any art and indeed like God, is not to be trammeled in the conceptual nets of proof and theory and formal demonstration. There is something deeply mysterious about two people becoming as one and yet remaining two distinct individuals, about two people growing and changing and developing and yet remaining stable and faithful within their commitments to one another. Sexual fidelity doesn't make any logical sense at all, and were reality commensurate with logic, then matrimony as I imagine it would be entirely illusory.

But in fact half of all marriages endure, and at least some of them are genuinely happy. Many of the divorced remarry, finding courage to try again despite what they have suffered. And some of these marriages are also genuinely happy. Satisfying, happy marriages are not an illusion, no matter how hard they are to understand. Storytelling is crucial to that understanding, I contend, because empirical sociological data are largely against us, as empirical data have always been "against" the spiritual journey and the quest for enlightenment.

Traditionally, of course, that quest is pursued by a solitary figure—commonly male—in isolation from social obligations and relationships. Traditionally, that quest is profoundly ascetic: The spiritual resonance of sexual delight is plainly ignored, just as the resonance of life with small children is ignored. The spiritual journey happens on the mountain or in the desert, not here in the suburbs. Sages don't peel carrots, wash socks, coach Little League, worry about downsizing, help with algebra, or save for college. But plenty of us do. As Keats insists in a different context, "Think not of them, thou hast thy music too."[8]

CHAPTER TWO

Erotic Desire
and Western Culture

Physical Appetite, Spiritual Need

Sexual arousal. Sexual delight, sexual drive, sexual instincts. Passion, climax, and release. How do we talk about such things? They arise from someplace stunningly prior to sentence construction and word choice, prior to argument and persuasion. But talk about it we do, by golly, just about endlessly: It is astounding how much has been said and written about human sexuality over the millennia. And thus there is no innocent beginning, no place to start that does not inevitably invoke other voices in this vast conversation.

Let me begin with one small, peppery observation. Sexual desire is different from other physical appetites in that it cannot be fully satisfied by the solitary individual. I can meet my need for food or for drink from a vending machine in an airport. I confess that in such situations I commonly relish a real Coca-Cola, one with both sugar and caffeine. It helps me get the plane into the air. In a pinch, I can still make do with those lurid, cellophane-wrapped "cheese" crackers with peanut butter. It's not ideal nutrition, and furthermore my fingertips turn orange. But it will do when the only alternative in the next eight hours will be those tiny bags of sugary peanuts handed out by flight attendants. And fortunately, Coke kills the taste of everything else. Of course food and drink can become deeply symbolic realities, and, furthermore, people eating alone can savour excellent cuisine. But the rudimentary biological need for calories and for fluids can effectively be satisfied from a machine in the middle of the night. I can sit and munch and watch the downpour or the blizzard, feeling deeply grateful for solid ground under my feet, and for peanut butter, and for the folks who resupply vending machines.

Sex just isn't like that. Real sexual desire cannot be satisfied on the cheap, no matter where life has stranded you. Cheap imitation sex, unlike cheap imitation food, does not quiet the hunger that desire involves, because sexual desire is far more than a simply physiological need. Sexual desire is powerfully and inevitably interwoven with the deepest levels of personal identity and with the most uncanny power of interpersonal relationships. Watch this progression: *Suppose that I want you in a sexual way. If so, then I also want you to want me in return. Furthermore, I want you to want me to want you.* And onward. As Rowan Williams explains, we all need our sexual desires to be reciprocated, and unless they are fully and richly reciprocated they cannot be entirely satisfied.[1] As a result, the vulnerabilities evoked by sexual desire are nothing short of stunning. We have no other physical need—food, sleep, shelter—that spirals so immediately and so deeply into the core questions all of us have about who we are. That is why sexually active relationships must also be faithful ones; that is why fidelity is such a crucial norm. "Desire" and "fidelity" name slightly different aspects of or perspectives on a single complex reality.

Where do we even begin to think about these issues? Should I begin by saying, "We are bodies," or should I start by saying, "We have bodies"? There's a difference. The small word change encodes a fundamental and vitally important philosophic and emotional distinction.[2] When you think "my *self*," when you think "*me*," do you think of your self as *inhabiting* a body, as a spirit or soul or psyche housed within muscle and bone? Or does "*me*" include your body in some deep, essential way?

"I Have a Body"

Is the "me-ness" of me essentially involved in or defined by this middle-aged body? Does the real *me* have such gray hair? What if I dyed my hair auburn again, took up aerobics, and developed graceful athletic abilities that (we may pretend) have lain dormant all these decades? Would doing so make a difference in my sense of self, my understanding or vision of myself? How? What if I merely quit drinking coffee? Don't you know people who claim that giving up caffeine or nicotine has changed their lives? People who started jogging, lost forty pounds, and felt very different about themselves?

When he was sixty-one William Butler Yeats lamented that

An aged man is but a paltry thing,
A tattered coat upon a stick, unless
Soul clap its hands and sing, and louder sing
For every tatter in its mortal dress.[3]

I know what Yeats means. I watched my father die slowly, month by month by month for years, day after day, watching his body in its inexorable decline toward death but seeing his spirit now and then crest above it all, bright and vital in its brief flashes. Even at the end, he was capable of one last distant but unmistakable revelation of a self that is transparently immortal, a spirit that is utterly and unquenchably what it has always been, undiminished by the body's decay. He had been comatose for weeks, but one afternoon he reached up and yanked the tube out of his nose. Blood spurted over both of us as I stood up and grabbed his hand.

"Ma was just here," he explained matter-of-factly, his morning-glory-blue eyes clear and confident and reassuring. "She told me I don't have to put up with this." His imitation of his mother's imperious tone was absolutely flawless, although she had been dead for more than ten years. It was one last great clap of the soul's hands, a faint but real twinkle in his eyes, a feeble shadow of his familiar, whimsical grin and shrug. He closed his eyes again and died a few hours later without further ado.

It was as close as I expect to come to immediate witnessing of the transcendent. At such moments it seems true to say, "I *have* a body," like having a house or having an apartment, like having a car that will get me thus far in my spiritual journey but no farther. Philosophically, such an understanding can be labeled "dualism." Essentially dualist arguments and positions run all through our thoughts about and attitudes toward sexual desire—especially the ways in which sex and death inevitably involve one another as complementary aspects of our progress from begotten to getting and then to gone. That's probably why "death" is an ancient poetic synonym for orgasm. Erotic arousal, like the very fact of our mortality, disrupts or at least complicates our ordinary sense of self.

"I Am a Body"

But there are other equally powerful and equally valid ways in which to frame the questions we have about sexual desire. Body and soul can be understood not as opposites but as a single complex entity; this tradition can be loosely called "wholistic."

My big Irish family collected itself last weekend for a party. All sorts of elderly or distant relations and extended-family friends were taken aback by how much my teenaged daughter, Carol, resembles me, how clearly she has my laugh and my smile and even my Murphy-clan green eyes. They kept hearing her voice in another room and thinking she was me. They were delighted; she was baffled and a bit annoyed. Here too are issues implicated in any definition of sexual desire.

We are each of us conceived in passion and born of a woman; we carry talents and traits, foibles and fingers that variously echo and allude to and work variations upon patterns from ancestors long, long forgotten. And in the fire of our own desires we can perpetuate that heritage, conceiving a child with her mother's voice but her father's golden hair. So I told Carol again the story of how, when she was a toddler, her frail and elderly great-uncle Bob, visiting from California, stood in the doorway in sudden tears at how much she looked like I had at that age. He took it as a blessing, I told her; he sat in the nearest chair and held out his arms to her. Inspired by some gracious angel, she went to him immediately without a word from anyone. He buried his face for a moment in her golden ringlets, and the room fell silent.

Sex is pretty incredible, I tried to explain to her. We are not found in the cabbage patch. We come into history; our sexuality is in part our encounter with the power and the capacity of community. We have a past and we have a future far beyond our mortal lives. But Carol was not impressed. She wants to be herself alone, her own face, her own voice. And I remember that feeling. But life is like this in big families and close-knit urban ethnic neighborhoods. My husband and my older sister's husband have gotten my sister and me confused at times; almost every relation at a further distance has given up remembering the slight differences between us. They just ask—as if we were identical twins, I suppose. And now she is delighted to be confused with a sister so much younger: Tables turn, in such matters, when you get past fifty.

Like that elderly uncle, we begin to find a certain comfort in the confounding fact that such a big clan seems to have only a couple of faces whose defining features we share and share about, generation after generation. My sister's dining room wall has a dozen framed portraits dating back a century; it looks as if the present generation spent an afternoon getting into and out of period costumes. Dye Tim's hair black and he could be his own great-great-grandfather on my father's side. That doesn't seem as claustrophobic a fact as it once did, and the maturity of those who adopt their children feels more and more like a profound moral achievement.

Dualist Versus Wholistic Visions of Embodiment

But physical resemblance is not just a source of family stories and stock jokes. It raises powerful questions about the connection between body and identity, body and mind, self and other—the answers to which provide the conceptual groundwork for any sexual ethics. When I was pregnant for the first time, I happened to be teaching René Descartes, the famous philosopher of dualism. One day I passed a most unruly afternoon: I was too big to hold a book without resting my forearms on the sides of my belly, but when I did so the baby pummeled my arms with such vigor that I could not concentrate. Concentrate on what? A French philosopher from the early seventeenth century who thought he could doubt the reality of his body but not the reality of his mind. Descartes, I realized, had never been pregnant. How might the history of philosophy change if he had been?

I set the book aside, locked my fingers atop my head to give this kid a rest from kicking me, and tried to imagine my way through Descartes's famous argument. I could not doubt the reality of my body. How could anyone? Had Descartes never been inconveniently hungry or distracted by arousal? Athletes, dancers, musicians, even test pilots, insist that our selves are bodies and our bodies are ourselves. We don't just rent space here. It's ours; it's us. That's really *me* there in the mirror, not just a mask or a container for my spirit. Physical performance of any kind, no less than pregnancy itself, is an encounter with the wholeness of the whole person, with the utter integrity of body and soul, with the resonance of Saint Paul's insistence upon the resurrection of the body.[4]

When we talk about sexual desire we are necessarily and inevitably engaging this whole complex question of embodiment, an enormous terrain variously mapped and explored, defined and delineated by intellectual ancestors no less potently real in us than our biological forebears. Contrary to the heritage of dualism, there is another ancestor, clearly subordinate but at some levels resurgent in the past fifty years— rather as my great-great-grandfather's flaming red hair finally showed up in my brother's daughter after so many generations of coppery brunettes. In this tradition, which we might call "wholistic," the self is not divided into mind versus body, thought versus passion. Nor—and this is a more subtle matter—is experience explained either as exclusively mental or as exclusively physical sensation.

In wholistic visions of embodiment, the locus of the ideal self is not the head but the heart (sometimes the viscera generally; sometimes the gut specifically), understood as the single unitary source of all the contents of consciousness.[5] The ideal is not intellectual self-control but rather a singleness or integrity that overcomes or precludes a divided heart, a forked tongue, or any other metaphoric vision of deceit or ambivalence or conflict, whether inward or outward. This ideal is said to be typical of at least some Native American traditions. It is also deeply characteristic of Hebrew scripture and thus central to the heritage of any of the Western monotheisms. It is evident, for instance, in the closing prayer for "gladness and singleness of heart" in *The Book of Common Prayer* used by Episcopalians[6] or in myriad references (in the Gospel of John and elsewhere) to the "peace that passes human understanding."

When we talk to our kids about sexual desire, when we try to explain sexual ethics to them under the pressure of their sharp questions, we inherit and engage and thereby conserve a Western moral tradition that is itself rich, complex, and many voiced. It has a lot to offer all of us. Above all, in the difficult conversations between parents and children, history offers what I think of as "rhetorical refuge." That is, history offers labels for various positions or attitudes, and history testifies to the consequences of these positions. We can make use of this history in our efforts to shift the basis of the discussion away from personalities and toward ideas.

In addition, we can at least begin to teach our children to identify and evaluate claims about sexuality, just as they are learning to evaluate advertising or politics or even movie reviews. These conversations about sex happen in little snippets over a period of years; even long-suffering kids like mine are unlikely to listen to complicated lectures on the history of sexual ethics. But if we have a clear historical and conceptual structure from which to respond to their remarks, then in time these scattered moments of trusting conversation will begin to assemble for them as much wisdom as we have to offer. With luck and with effort, we can not only respond to their remarks but also—albeit casually and not too often—make carefully pointed observations of our own about the sexuality we observe around us.

Nonetheless, let's remember that no one comes to terms with sexuality just by thinking about ideas and traditions. These issues are deep in our guts and only partly conscious at best. We need to remember that and—when push comes to shove—trust our guts to speak a truth that we ignore at our peril. As we review the contradictory abundance of our cultural heritage, we must above all remember and respect the ways in which "I am a body" and "I have a body" name very real tensions within everyone's experience. Both explanations "work" at least some of the time for all us, but neither works all the time for anyone. Simplicity is suspect because the reality is not only complex but also genuinely mysterious.

We are two, my body and I, a soul that is learning to clap its hands. And I am one, just me here, really embodied and not just renting space, coppery hair gone so gray that in the pictures from my niece's wedding last October I look just like the picture of my Grandma Murphy taken at my parents' wedding. (Carol called the two snapshots "seriously weird.") A workable sexual ethics must take both dimensions of self-experience into account.

Wholistic Views of Sexuality: Sigmund Freud

Western thought about sexual desire can be imagined on a continuum anchored at one end by Sigmund Freud and at the other by Saint Augustine of Hippo. Freud argued from the wholistic, or "I am a body," perspective. He explained that originally, or in childhood, sexual drives are manifested as a diffuse orientation toward particular kinds of somatic pleasure. Only gradually does the child's pervasive and unconscious erotic delight in almost everything get itself organized under and focused upon the functions of reproduction.[7]

I was a bit dubious about Freud's argument until I had children of my own. Then I could see for myself what Freud was pointing out. There is no mistaking the depth of physical pleasure a baby enjoys in whatever it finds pleasing. Babies welcome parents with a smile that is a whole-body response, not something merely of the face. Toddlers gleefully smoosh peas or curds of cottage cheese one by one by one. No sensual delight is too minute to escape their notice: As a toddler, Mark would gently stroke the new growth on the arborvitae at the park and enjoy its fragrance. I could almost hear the tree purring in response. For years we could not walk by that hedge without pausing for the solemn exchange of greetings between boy and tree. It doesn't demand uncommon empathic gifts to intuit the as yet unconscious and undeveloped origins of such intense delight in all the beauties of creation. Freud's hostility to religion notwithstanding, the world is indeed holy, and we are born in tune with it.

Life with babies illustrated for me how true it is that sexuality underlies or funds all sensuality of any kind, and sensuality is merely the experience of being bodies. That's why sex sells cars or toothpaste or even mutual funds. That's how silk long underwear, flannel sheets, and ruby-red grapefruit get me through January. That's why thousands of people stood five abreast in line in the August sun for four hours to get into the recent Monet exhibit at the Art Institute of Chicago. If you can't feel the erotic dimension of your own response to something like Cousin Ellen's light, spicy pumpkin mousse pie, I'm inclined to worry that you are just not paying attention. All such delight, however deeply matured (or "sublimated") from the baby's diffuse sexuality, nonetheless still resonates all the way down to our deepest biological and psychological drives. Sexual pleasure per se, sexual desire as such, is merely the focusing upon reproductive function of the central delight we have in being alive, the joy of bodies that are alive and well and loose in the cosmos.

All energy is bodily energy, even the energy spent upon the most abstruse questions in mathematics. And all bodily energy arises within consciousness from our delight in body and our psychic organization around the seeking of such delight. In a mature or well-developed personality, only a portion of that energy is consciously erotic, of course. From the wholistic perspective, erotic desire is in itself neither good nor bad, although it can be developed and integrated in good ways or in bad ways, in healthy ways or in destructive ways. I am heterosexual and female and somewhat slight of build. I can be happy and healthy, well integrated and productive at being this way. Or I can be miserable or crazy or violent or repressed. But no amount of effort on my part can make me someone different, someone taller or bigger or differently oriented sexually. Such things are, as they say, "hardwired" into the selves that we are.

The Corruption of Wholistic Views: Hedonism

Sexual ethics from a wholistic perspective asks how successfully the conscious erotic drives have been integrated into the well-developed personality, or into the whole of one's identity. That's a difficult philosophical and psychological question about a massively complex process. In the face of such hard questions, our first-level "answer," particularly in recent decades, has been to cop out altogether. The challenge of real integration loses out to the simplicity of hedonism. If it feels good, do it.

This credo was the cheerful, libidinous premise of the "sexual revolution." Anything less than wholehearted, immediate gratification was labeled "repression" or "neurosis." Shabby, even sleazy pop psychologies misappropriated a technical psychodynamic vocabulary in the service of claims that boiled down to nothing more than exploitative self-indulgence. *As long as nobody gets hurt,* goes the qualifying clause, *as long as nobody gets hurt,* everyone's life and everyone's psychic development were said to be served by the unbridled gratification of sexual desires.

The problem, of course, is that people do get hurt. They probably always get hurt, although we may not see the injury easily. This kind of unrestrained self-indulgence proves terribly self-destructive in the end, as my baby boom generation rediscovered the hard way. "Free love," like its next of kin "recreational drugs," proves to be neither fun nor free in the end.

Dan, for instance. Danny. He had a very long, thin face, and his head seemed not a fraction wider than his neck. Only his smile disrupted the long vertical line, a smile so wide it seemed liable to snap his head off just below his nose—a rather generous nose for such a thin face. His hair was so straight it wouldn't curve to lie flat along his head. It grew down like a kindergarten portrait from some single point on the top of his head. Dan was a mathematician—a prodigy, some kids said—cruising through advanced courses even as a freshman and getting the math faculty very excited. We would collect around the blackboard in the Honors House to listen to Dan talk, long, thin Dan gesturing like a pterodactyl holding chalk in its wingtip and cracking that incredible smile. We never actually dated, but Dan would reliably swoop down beside me with a great-winged one-arm hug. He liked poetry too, and he knew far more about it than I have ever grasped of real mathematics.

Sophomore year, Dan got involved with the kids dropping acid. That did not matter to me at first. I had a wide array of friends, because I did not take sides in the bitter arguments over dinner about whether recreational drugs were nothing more than our generation's version of the booze our parents drank. Marijuana smoke set off my asthma so unbearably that I could not go to the parties where it was commonplace. If someone lit a joint—or even a "real" cigarette—I was in trouble pretty quickly. So my allergies were an exemption of sorts: I stayed away from both their parties and their arguments. Furthermore, I had inherited such a slight frame that I had minimal tolerance for the cheap red wine that was popular in other circles. I drank one glass and maybe part of a second, very slowly and with lots of food: Everyone realized that this was physiology, not virtue.

And so I was that useful resource, the person reliably sober. Kids sometimes had very bad reactions, whether from the LSD or from contaminants none of us knew. But "bad trips" were not uncommon, even among those merely smoking pot. Kids who were hallucinating needed lots of protection and attention; afterward they needed a chance to talk their way through the lingering anxiety. They needed to be more or less "supervised" for a few days, escorted to and from classes, taken to meals. One way and another, I was at least on the fringes of that care pretty regularly.

One night some people came to me about Danny. He had been on a bad trip for three days, and he wasn't coming out of it. He had been shifted from one floor to another in the biggest women's dorm, walked up and down and up and down in the hallways when resident advisers were out to class, fed with what girls could sneak out of the cafeteria. They had tried everything they knew to sober him up. But he didn't look good, and he was looking worse as the hours passed. He was having more and more trouble walking. He'd quit talking, not even nonsense. Some wanted to call his parents, some to take him to an emergency room, some to just keep walking him and hoping. Everyone was accusing everyone else of arguing what they would want for themselves in his situation. So they came to me. They trusted my allergies to keep me innocent: I wouldn't have an opinion for myself but rather for Dan. I sat on my bed, wrapped in my bathrobe, and listened.

As the argument surged back and forth, consensus built fairly rapidly toward calling his parents. Maybe it was better for them to hear from his friends than from some hospital clerk. Besides, if they found illegal drugs in his system, Danny might need not only a doctor but also a lawyer. They called his folks, and Dan was hustled surreptitiously down the block to a guys' dorm so somebody could get him into the shower before his parents arrived from the airport.

Dan disappeared after that for about a year. Then he re-enrolled, dropped out promptly, and got a job delivering newspapers. At first he had had a clerical job in the delivery-service office, kids said, but he just couldn't handle the numbers. So he delivered papers instead, carrying tidy stacks of them in a big canvas sling on his narrow, sloping shoulder. He would sit around on the steps of the student union all afternoon, sometimes with the morning papers still in his bag. His eyes were bright but he was gone. I hugged this bony shell of a man and felt utterly hopeless. No less than the Kennedys or King or the deaths at Kent State, the demise of Danny is for me an event that defined both the age and my own slow coming-of-age. Would it have made a difference if I had saddled my fear that night and insisted that Dan be taken immediately to the university hospital downtown? I don't know.

It's fun, went those endless arguments over dinner in the cafeteria. It's just fun, and nobody gets hurt unless somebody calls the cops. Except sometimes. Like the "sometimes" pregnancies. I know stories like that too. I know many more stories about unexpected pregnancies than I know of unexpected trouble with illegal drugs—despite living amidst the university student drug culture from 1968, when I graduated from high school, until 1977, when I finished my Ph.D. I suspect that almost everyone in my generation knows "bad pregnancy" tales. We have been there and we have done that, or at least seen it, more or less. We know about lives as devastated by casual sex as Danny's was by drugs. But stories about sexual misadventures and unwanted pregnancies are harder to tell than Dan's tale because they are longer and less materially conclusive. The tragedies spin out over decades—perhaps generations. It would take an Anne Tyler to tell the story well.

When Tim was in kindergarten, one of his friends asked to sit in Warren's lap.

"I don't have a dad," Tod explained. "My mom never got one. I just want to try it out." Warren cuddled him for a minute or two; then he got down and ran off to play with a "thanks" and a nod as if Warren had handed him a cookie. Tod is still round faced and pink cheeked, even as a teenager. And he is getting himself into increasingly serious trouble. I don't know the story, but if you could see his eyes you wouldn't need the details. Besides, chances are that your kids also have friends more or less like Tod, or friends whose custodial parents have had endless strings of lovers, or friends whose custodial residences change, and change back, and change again as the parents battle ongoing emotional chaos in their own lives. Maybe we fooled our parents, at least a lot of the time. But we have not hidden the facts from our children. And so we fund programs to harangue them, to browbeat them, to indoctrinate them with antisex, antidrug rock tunes, as if morality could be marketed and our own vague and guilty ambivalences resolved by good computer graphics and a synthesized bass line.

Such simpleminded repression is no better than the simpleminded hedonism it mirrors so precisely. Furthermore, we are insisting that their immediate, powerful emotional needs and impassioned personal relationships must be sacrificed to their individual long-term earning potential and career progress. I do not dispute that pregnancy can interfere catastrophically with a teenager's education and so forth. But I worry about what this incessant, high-volume indoctrination will reap when our children discover, perhaps decades from now, that having children and caring faithfully for children even in one's thirties will interfere with maximizing income and professional advancement. And I worry that our children hear these messages as explanations of why they do not have more of our time and attention. Are we teaching them that children as such are onerous burdens who interfere with parents' careers? That relationships—with sexual partners or with children—must be sacrificed to economic ambition? That they matter less to us than money? Children listen far more intently and think far more consistently and honestly than many adults realize. Cost-benefit sex ed programs are not secular at all: They teach the worship of careers or money above all other gods. And when the religious alternatives are either theologically arcane or simply repressive—or both—then we have ourselves one fine predicament.

Gleefully hedonist gratification is not the same as mature integration. Sexuality is far too intimate a part of our identities to be managed merely as an appetite, as something not qualitatively different from a taste for Oreos or ruby-red grapefruit. Like Danny, we risk everything we are. We may not appreciate the risk until it is far too late. But when we start thinking that we need to subordinate sexual drives as such to something else, then we have crossed the boundary into "I have a body" experiences. And then the question becomes, Subordinate to what? *Subordinate to intellect* has been the usual Western response, philosophically labeled "hierarchical dualism." Intellect and body are two separate things, and intellect ought to rule body.

Dualist Views of Sexuality: Augustine of Hippo

Among dualist schemes of sexual ethics, a classic or central figure is Augustine of Hippo.[8] Augustine was an important Christian theologian who lived from 354 to 430 C.E.—that is, in the very last decades of late classical antiquity. (He died during the Vandal siege of his city in North Africa.) Saint Augustine was a Manichaeist before his famous conversion to Christianity in 386–387 C.E. He came to oppose Manichaeism, but nonetheless it profoundly influenced much of his thought about sexuality.

Manichaeism was a widely influential and radically dualist religion in late antiquity. It taught that mind or intellect or spirit is good, and matter or body—all of physical creation—is evil. The physical universe is or represents or enacts the rebellion or incursion of evil; in the triumph of good at end-time, physical reality will evaporate back into the nothingness it has always been for the enlightened observer. Meanwhile, sexual intercourse is sinful because of the overwhelming physical pleasure of orgasm and because the material world itself is extended by the birth of a child. In telling this story, Manes drew together elements from a variety of religions in the ancient world, both from the Mediterranean basin and from India, synthesizing them within a centrally Greek and gnostic conceptual structure. Eventually, orthodox Christianity declared that Manichaeism and Manichaeist versions of Christianity were heretical.

Augustine acknowledged that sexual pleasure is "a pleasure unsurpassed among those of the body. The effect of this is that at the very moment of its climax there is an almost total eclipse of acumen and, as it were, sentinel alertness." But in his account there is something degrading, even terrifying, about that eclipse of intellect. Nor is the loss of control at orgasm the only problem. Erections can be neither summoned nor banished by the intellect: "At times the urge intrudes uninvited; at other times it deserts the panting lover and although desire is ablaze in the mind, the body is frigid."[9]

And so, he decided, "surely any friend of wisdom and holy joys . . . would prefer, if he could, to beget children without this kind of lust. . . . It is reasonable then that we should feel very much ashamed of such lust, and reasonable too that those members which it moves or does not move by its own right, so to speak, and not in full subjection to our will, should be called pudenda or shameful parts."[10]

He speculated that our degrading subjection to these rebellious parts of our bodies constitutes our punishment for rebelling against God in Eden: Because we rebelled against God, we are forced to endure the humiliations imposed by bodies that rebel against us. Were it not for original sin, he suggested, a man could beget a child with the same serene self-possession with which he might sprinkle seeds in the garden.[11] Adam and Eve would have conceived children in Eden had they remained obedient, he decided, but they would have been able to do so without sexual intercourse.[12]

It is tempting to laugh at the idea that orgasm constitutes punishment for sin. It's not exactly clear, at least in our day, how this state of affairs might be construed as discouraging further disobedience. But we do not share Augustine's unquestioned assumption that even a momentary loss of intellectual, willful self-control is innately shameful and humiliating—and perhaps more intensely so for Augustine than for most of his contemporaries. For Augustine, the "self" was intellect and the body was "it," the body was "other." The body's overwhelming pleasure in and subjection to arousal was a shameful thing that needed to be studied and explained as an objective affliction.

The power of sexual arousal could be depicted as humiliating because self-control was, in Augustine's world, as commonplace and as commonly unexamined a value as self-expression is in ours. In our day, most people simply take it for granted that we seek self-expression and that impediments to self-expression are painful. Most people would never think to ask why or stop to defend the presupposition that everyone ought to "contribute to discussion." (Introverts may ask, I suppose, but we are a tiny minority that is easily shouted down.) In fact, Augustine was merely presupposing the commonplace value of self-control, not arguing for it. His major argument was a refutation of the very powerful Manichaeists. Augustine sought not so much to "repress" sexuality as to define its legitimacy by defending the role of sexual procreation—even if sanitized of orgasm— in Eden, in the best or original order of the cosmos.

It is tempting to take Augustine out of historical context and then to blame him, and to blame his Christian heirs, for the whole history of sexual repression and sexual obsession in the West. But that's not fair, and it's not accurate, and above all it confuses the Christian spiritual heritage from the Jews with our philosophic heritage from the Greeks and from the Hellenized culture of the Mediterranean basin. But the truth remains that Christians worship neither Zeus nor Socrates but rather Yahweh of the Jews as understood by Jesus of Nazareth.

Augustine is representative of how the early Christian church used the best conceptual tools at its disposal as it struggled to decide whether or not it was essentially Jewish. Maybe "Christianity" was a new religion. Or maybe Christians were schismatics from Judaism—something like a foreshadowing of the later schism of Protestants from Roman Catholicism. (Theologians still argue about Christianity and the Jews, sometimes quite hotly.) But to be a new religion, to be a universal religion in late antiquity meant being a religion with an essentially Greek conceptual structure and psychology. And that meant one or another version of mind-over-body duality such as we see in Manichaeism. Hierarchical dualism was—more or less—the popular psychology of late antiquity, perfectly evident in other major ethical movements such as Stoicism and Cynicism.[13]

Augustine realized that in his world, the goodness of sexuality needed defending or justifying in ways that now strike us as quaint—or maybe even bizarre. As the Roman empire slowly collapsed, the times were strange and difficult and increasingly chaotic. It is vital to realize—as thinkers of the Dark and Middle Ages often did not—that the wisdom of the past can be appropriated only after it has been carefully and precisely resituated in the human context of its own time and authorship. I am, then, in some ways plainly and directly the heiress of Augustine in my attempt to redeem the value and dignity of sexuality from Manichaeism—like him keeping one eye on the best psychology of my own time, which argues that sexuality must be wisely integrated within the dynamics of the individual psyche.

Dualist Sexual Ethics and the Problem of Orgasm

Under the pressure of time and circumstance, the complex and contradictory early Christian heritage was ground down and reread and corrupted into the slurry of popular culture and politics that comprised medieval "Christendom." As modernity has seen pseudointellectual defenses of hedonism, the Middle Ages saw pseudointellectual defenses of pious Manichaeism: Mind is good but body is bad; men and abstract intellect are pure and powerful; women and sensuality or feelings are both degenerate and inferior; celibate men are morally superior to married men because they are more removed from contamination by the erotic and the feminine. In this ideology, God is imagined exclusively as the Father Almighty, a Heavenly King who is no less "remote, serene,

and indifferent" than the Platonic nous; "He" is utterly incapable of feelings of any sort—except, of course, murderous
rage thinly disguised as rationalist opposition to all that is
sensual and passionate within humanity.

Set forth as bluntly as this, the ideas are obviously wrong
and transparently indefensible.[14] That weakness seldom
makes much of a difference, especially when the falsehood
translates so easily for some into political power and gender
privilege. Like hedonism, I suspect, repressive internal hier-
archies are among the perennially recurring illusions or idol-
atries to which human culture is prone. And of course there
have always been prophetic denunciations of such evil, in the
Middle Ages no less than in our own time.

For centuries, then, procreation was regarded as the sole
legitimate expression of mature erotic sexuality; in other
contexts, orgasm was wrong. Furthermore, procreative sexual acts, even within marriage, were regarded as very probably the occasion of sins such as concupiscence and lust, so the
faithful were enjoined from sex on Sundays and holy days,
during Lent and Advent, and so forth. Infertile and elderly
married couples were enjoined from sexual relations altogether. As late as the nineteenth century, Roman Catholic
theologians recount, official guides for priests hearing confessions still held that rape and incest were lesser sexual sins
than masturbation because they had procreative potential.[15]

Of course, parish clergy and their congregations were regularly chastised from distant palaces for failing to hew to such
guidelines: There is a rich, albeit subterranean, heritage of compassion, common sense, and double-thinking. When I was in
high school in the mid-'60s, for instance, one of the nuns
(still wearing long medieval garb) spent a week teaching us
the advantages, disadvantages, and failure rates of every con-
traceptive on the market. She drew IUDs on the blackboard,

explained how to apply spermicide to diaphragms, and discussed various formulations of the Pill. There were no tests and no written materials and no one who was not paying very close attention. We were not to take notes; our desks had to be clear.

She began each class with a sharp admonition that it is morally wrong to conceive more children than you can properly nurture and provide for. She ended each class with a fast, flat, rote admonition that contraception was still officially— although not "infallibly"—forbidden, which meant we needed the permission of a priest. It was exactly like the "fine print" recited at incomprehensible speed by radio announcers. More than once I made the good sister blush by watching her too closely during this final speech. She was doing graduate work in theology at the University of Chicago, and we decided that she had probably learned all this stuff there, in a "public" school.

The daring of that nun might become more clear if I explain that in Oak Park, where I grew up, families of eight to ten children were roughly the norm. A family wasn't considered unusually big until there were more than a dozen kids. Almost every family had a child in almost every grade: My siblings and I still keep the big neighborhood clans straight by reciting the names of the kids in birth order, then remembering which kid shared a grade with which of us. It's the Irish equivalent of Protestant kids reciting the books of the Bible in order. It's why Irish wakes and Italian weddings go on for so long: Nobody goes home until everyone has placed everyone else, with their husbands and wives and kids. That can take a while: One of my mother's best friends has twenty grandchildren and another eighty great- or great-great-grandchildren. And most of them still live in the neighborhood.

When we buried my dad, my oldest brother counted seventy families that came in family groups that spanned four generations; for two days people stood three and four abreast in a line that wound out the front door and around the corner toward the parking lot of the funeral parlor. The recitals of names felt like something out of Homer, like the endless "begats" of the Bible. In such a world I accepted at face value my parents' apologetic stance in the community for having had "only" five children in twelve years. My mother repeatedly explained and apologized to me for what she understood as her fertility problems. My brothers and sister and I worked hard, I suspect, to make up for being so few in number. When I was small, "only five" seemed seriously deficient.

Nonetheless, our parish was a liberal community. The women were outraged by the Pope's attempt to continue the ban on birth control in despite of his own theologians; they did not want my generation to suffer as they had suffered. In the face of such powerful confidence from these women sitting around my mother's kitchen, I did not truly appreciate the very real threat posed to my teacher and to my school by the conservative and authoritarian hierarchy at the diocesan mansion downtown. I thought the nun's top-secret style was silly and degrading for all of us. Surely, I thought, Protestant kids are taught this stuff in the public schools all the time. Surely Protestants can discuss the disadvantages of condoms more easily than this. But I had never met a Protestant kid, so I had no one to ask.

More importantly, of course, I had no appreciation of how dramatically the Reformation had reaffirmed the ancient dualist disapproval of sexual passion and physical pleasure of any kind. The Calvinists, the Puritans, the Lutherans—these folks are not known for their relaxed sensuality and joie de vivre. As the Reformation spun out into the Enlightenment, Protestant Europe saw a truly savage recurrence of violence and hatred directed against women—especially young women—and a correlative resurgent distrust of emotion and sensuality generally.

Dualist Christianity—on either side of the Reformation—condemns homosexuality for the same reason it condemns birth control: as a perversion of the "natural law" that orgasm is wrong unless that pleasure redeems itself by the potential for procreation. Homosexual unions are not potentially procreative, just like heterosexual unions among the infertile, the postmenopausal, and those using contraception. If sex has to make babies (at least potentially) to make the grade morally, a lot of us are going to be in big trouble sooner or later. And the woes of working-class Irish communities fade in comparison to the starvation, disease, and violence in the Third World—suffering that is in no small way consequent upon skyrocketing populations. (I left the Roman Catholic church after a copy of Ehrlich and Ehrlich, *Population, Resources, Environment: Issues in Human Ecology* made its way from hand to hand in my undergraduate Jesuit college.)[16]

Procreativity is not a warrant of sexual morality. Rape can be procreative. Incest can be procreative. Prostitution can be procreative. Procreation establishes fertility, not morals. What guarantees morality is the human relationship in which the sexual act is situated. Homosexuality can be moral or immoral in exactly the same ways and for exactly the same reasons as heterosexuality. Bathhouses are just as bad as brothels, and genuine sexual fidelity is not dependent upon orientation. All of us are called to a single common standard of morality in sexual relationships as in personal relationships generally: Integrity is a universal norm. Fidelity is a norm applicable to everyone, straight and gay alike.

Sexual orientation exempts no one from the demands of sexual fidelity, nor does it exclude anyone from matrimony in the sacramental sense. Long-standing sacramental doctrine in the high or liturgical Christian churches insists that the sacrament of matrimony is administered by one partner to the other. The sacrament is witnessed by the priest or minister and by the congregation but is not administered by the cleric. And what is witnessed, more often than not, is the serious and committed intention to struggle toward achieving that full sacramental union. Full sacramental matrimony develops gradually, as every long-married couple knows. Outsiders can choose to acknowledge and support that process or to deny and impede it, but we can neither create nor allow the sacramental reality of anyone else's marriage. That's up to God, not us.

We do not control the power to bless or refuse to bless homosexual unions: Partners in any matrimonial alliance bless one another, and they are blessed by God. As a community we have only the power publicly or communally to teach and to support the moral value of honorable and committed sexual fidelity and just as powerfully and clearly to oppose the travesties of promiscuous, predatory, exploitative sexuality. If churches are going to expend energy worrying about sex—rather than poverty or hunger or homelessness or war—that energy ought to be expended on the distinctions that matter. Orientation is not the distinction that matters. Fidelity is.

The important threat to heterosexual unions is not homosexual unions but heterosexual infidelity and failures or breakdowns of intimacy between husbands and wives. Acknowledging faithful and committed homosexual unions can threaten family life and the stable nurture of children only if we are led thereby, as a society, to regard marriage with greater casualness than we already do. But I'm not sure that greater casualness is possible when adultery is widely described as "commonplace" or as a "minor sexual misbehavior."[17] The crucial task before us in these days is to reflect seriously on how we can help each other to sustain fidelity within matrimony and to teach sexual ethics to our children.

In this regard I am particularly worried about the plight of homosexual teenagers, who commit suicide in terrifying numbers. Parents of gay and lesbian youths are no less worried than the rest of us that their kids will be devastated both emotionally and physically by promiscuity. And yet the religious right in effect tells these kids that they are innately, irredeemably depraved and incapable of sexually faithful and committed relationships. But parents know—or discover—that loyal and honorable kids are still just as loyal and honorable, just as kind and decent, just as loving and just as beloved after they find themselves to be homosexual. These kids must not be abandoned by their families, by their friends, and by their communities. Of course, they will need particular role models of mature sexual ethics from among the ranks of steadfastly faithful gay or lesbian couples, but first and foremost they need to know that they still "belong" under all the familiar norms of sexual fidelity upheld by the heterosexual adults they have always loved and idealized.

The brother of one of my dearest friends is dying of AIDS in San Francisco; his faithful partner of many years died about eighteen months ago. His parents won't see him, won't acknowledge his sexual orientation, won't even admit that he is dying. My friend is devastated not only by her brother's slow decline into dementia and death but also by her parents' betrayal of him and, indirectly, of her. She lives in a notoriously conservative region, and she is afraid to tell her friends—even her friends at her church or her pastor—that her beloved younger brother is dying of AIDS and has been abandoned by her parents. She is afraid her grief will be scorned and her children stigmatized. The most she can manage is an occasional long-distance phone conversation with me.

This is not an uncommon story in our day. It has everything to do with the mix of sexuality and morality—but orientation is not what's called into question.

Individualism and the Sexual "Market"

So Freud and Augustine, corrupted into hedonism and repression, anchor the extremes of the continuum as I imagine it. What's the middle ground? How do most sensible people think about sex and talk about sex in our own day? American popular culture seeks to integrate sexual desire into its own dominant metaphor, the marketplace. Implicitly or explicitly, we imagine something like a social market within which each person seeks to satisfy sexual drives and to remedy the loneliness attendant upon modern American individualism.[18] Appropriate sexual relationships, according to popular American culture, reveal the implicit presence of a good, clean contract. That is, both partners agree openly and fully to the terms and the duration of their relationship.

Marketplace sexuality is profoundly hedonist in its emphasis on one's own pleasure as the greatest good. Yet it is also more profoundly dualist than anything Augustine might ever have imagined, because sexual feelings and needs are "managed" so as to "optimize return." Marketplace metaphors for sexual relationships are powerful because they reconcile profoundly different trends in Western culture by drawing on the worst aspects of each and imagining our most vulnerable depths as the objects of barter.

Such relationships are not for better and for worse but only for as long as the relationship is fulfilling or fun or self-enhancing. It's management hedonism: I exploit you, but not too much; you exploit me, but not too much. The bottom line, the spreadsheet, has to stay balanced, and it's that vision of quid-pro-quo balance that makes marketplace sexuality inherently exploitative.

Adam Smith aside, it is not true that the greatest good of the whole society is achieved by the absolutely ruthless pursuit by each individual of his or her own individual good, constrained only by the resistance of other equally powerful, equally ruthless individuals. We reap what we sow and nothing better: a ruthlessly exploitative society in which disparities of power or status are catastrophic. Children, who are both needy and poor competitors, are scandalously neglected; honor, duty, respect, kindness, and morality restrain very few people in any serious public way. Might may not make right, but it has always defined "right" quite successfully. As bureaucratic institutions, the Christian churches can be as exploitative and exclusionary as other profoundly hierarchical social structures. Nonetheless, they conserve and sometimes honestly employ powerful symbolic resources and an ample conceptual language whereby to depict such behavior as morally wrong and as neither inevitable nor necessary. What hope there may be for meaningful social reform probably resides somewhere within this difficult set of paradoxes regarding religion in American culture.

In the world as we have it, we cannot solve the problem of mutual exploitation by imposing a legal requirement that sexual partners must first procure a marriage license from the state, as if they were about to plant a shrub in the vicinity of buried utility lines or perhaps remodel the front porch. Communal witness to the initiation of a commitment is genuinely valuable—if the couple already belongs to a community that understands and supports sexual commitment. But lots of good people have not found such a community. Whether or not they throw a fancy party or register for housewares, however, most couples will at least turn to their good friends and close family for recognition and support of the risky decision to make such a commitment. Public or legal witness remains important for those with significant resources, so as to establish clear property rights, and for those who are planning pregnancies, so as to establish the rights and obligations of the father; but legal formalities seem now to be a stage in a committed relationship rather than the first step. The fact remains that licensing an exploitative relationship doesn't make it less exploitative. It just makes it legal.

Divorce rates, divorce law, widespread adultery, and the reality of both catastrophic promiscuity and catastrophic marriages demonstrate that what we need in talking to our kids is to articulate a vision of matrimonial fidelity that is deeply grounded in a sophisticated, wholistic understanding of our humanity. We need an alternative vision to decadent Western dualisms, whether those of the religious right or those of the cost-benefit sexual marketplace encoded by the radical individualism of popular culture. These sophistries—not homosexuality—are the real threats to the development and maintenance of matrimony and the stable nurture of children.

Talking to Teens About Desire

It's tough to talk about sex with teens, but a lot of that difficulty is not our fault. Our teenagers have an enormous psychodynamic need to remain oblivious to the possibility of our having any such thing as sexual desire. But we do talk to our children regularly about the problem of embodiment. We don't call it that, of course. We call it "Take a shower," or

"Go to bed," or "Don't eat that now; dinner is in three minutes." Parents and kids are engaged with the problems of embodiment beginning with that first night home from the hospital with a baby who has not yet mastered the skill of settling down to sleep or eating heartily. Parents of toddlers and teens alike oppose hedonism on a daily basis. Teenagers don't eat crayons, of course, and toddlers do not have to be counseled against buying pizza and french fries for lunch every day at school. But the issues are not particularly different—except I suppose that ordinary kids eat more greasy junk than crayons.

A kid who has a reasonable grasp of his own embodied desires generally will have a solid emotional foundation from which to begin to engage the more complicated desire of sexual arousal. Above all, I think, a kid whose parents have responded gently and wisely to his or her accounts of appetites in general will prove to be a kid who can ask the slight, off-the-cuff questions with which teenagers begin conversations about sex. Because we have responded compassionately to their physical needs for all of their lives, they count on us for some wisdom in their self-regulation of this particular and highly charged need. I've tried to offer some of that wisdom here by coming at the issue historically and by offering a historical sketch that parents can use in framing for themselves the issues their kids raise in that scattershot way. I'm convinced that once we free sexuality from the guilt-ridden slough of repressive Western dualisms and from the exploitative excesses of individualism, we will find it easier both to think about sexual desire judiciously for ourselves and to begin to reason with our kids by analogy to other desires that they have already begun to integrate within the whole of who they are.

CHAPTER THREE

Intimacy in Relationships

Casual Sex

I argued throughout the preceding chapter, in various ways, that sexual desire is far more than a simple physiological need. Sexual desire is powerfully and intricately interwoven with the deepest levels of human identity and with the most difficult questions we have about who we are or what it means to be human. Sexual desire can be repressed, or it can be heedlessly indulged, or it can become a calculated part of a marketplace exchange. Or, I will propose in this chapter, sexual desire can be integrated into the whole of who we are. The question, of course, is *how.* How or where does sexual desire "belong" in the whole that we are?

The answer demands a return to my initial observation about sexual desire: It cannot be genuinely satisfied on the cheap or by the solitary individual. At its most potent, most vital, most delightful levels, sexual desire must be reciprocated to be sated. That's why we cannot "locate" an appropriate sexuality without considering the human relationship in which it is realized or enacted. We need to know the basis of the interaction in which sexual intercourse participates. Is it really mutual, for instance? Are both partners offering and seeking the same things? Consider rape, or prostitution, or the sexual abuse of a child. Consider how sexual access has been demanded as a condition of employment, promotion, business contracts, or social acceptance. The disparities are self-evident. It's easy to see what's wrong, which is a first step toward articulating an appropriate sexual relationship.

It may not be as easy to see what is wrong with what I have called "marketplace" sexual ethics. Consider this scenario, for instance: Two adults meet at one of those exhausting and tedious professional meetings held in banal hotels near the airports of cold, bleak cities. After three days of grueling seminars predicting the imminent collapse of the industry that employs them, they decide to join a few friends in skipping the Annual Self-Congratulatory Dinner. They pile themselves into a couple of cabs and head off for real food somewhere remote from the peculiar antiseptic smell of big hotels. They share a meal and a few drinks, grousing and joking and telling stories in the usual friendly way of bored and lonely strangers at meetings. En route back to the hotel, the two people we are watching find themselves distinctly enjoying the physical attraction that has buzzed about the edges of their interactions over the last few hours and days. They linger in the lobby as the group disperses, quite aware that they are very attracted to one another.

There is the possibility here of a free, independent sexual exchange between mature adults who are equal to one another in age, status, and so forth: just tonight, no strings, no phone calls later, no promises, and no regrets. Good contraception, let us suppose. Safe sex. Privacy assured. Suppose both are single and neither is willing to consider a permanent relationship. Or suppose they are, both of them, actively looking for life partners; or suppose one is. Or suppose one or both are married. Under any of these circumstances, is a casual sexual encounter OK?

My short answer in any of these situations is *no*, and my long answer is the burden of this chapter. Casual sexual encounters are morally wrong because the exchange is partial even when it is entirely equal or open or honest. Sex in these situations is not genuinely reciprocal but rather mutually exploitative and, ultimately, mutually self-denigrating. In such an exchange, each regards his or her own sexual desire as a primarily physiological need essentially separable from the deeper psychological and emotional union that is physically enacted in sexual intercourse. I contend that we cannot split ourselves into parts like that.

Body and heart or soul are one. Any attempt to dissociate them is both doomed and dangerous, and that is how casual sex injures even free and willing participants. It severs vital connections within the self, thereby silencing or at least muting one of the most powerful and literally vital foundations of our richest and most creative relationships with other people. Casual sex easily devastates the capacity for serious sex.

This risk remains inescapable even if the sex is much less casual than this imaginary encounter between people who have known each other only briefly. I contend that we are not wise to regard sexual intercourse as an essentially ordinary and acceptable expression of affection between men and women who have made no permanent commitment to one another. Of course, many people will disagree with me, in effect arguing that sexual desire can be merely an appetite or a friendly gesture in some relationships and yet still retain its role as the symbolic embodiment of commitment when they are ready to make that sort of commitment. The disagreement has less to do with sex, I believe, than with the philosophy of symbol and the psychology of symbolic expression and perception—which leads quickly into complex theories of imagination and creativity.

Those woods are lovely, dark and deep; let me but steal a twig and then keep going. I said at the beginning that sexual fidelity is an art, and like all arts it is dependent upon disciplines and practices learned and sustained over time and within communities. Let me take that idea one step further. These disciplines and practices—and especially the most embodied or material and "technical" of them—provide the crucial foundation for symbolic perception and expression. The glorious coherence and lucidity and passion of a fine musical performance are not possible except through years of excruciating discipline, both in the exact actions of fingers or other parts of the body and in the detailed material and technical aspects of music and musical composition. Literature too involves an array of word choices and technical strategies that critics spend lifetimes trying to understand and to appreciate. The art that is sexual fidelity also depends upon a deeply complex, not fully conscious array of spiritual and material aesthetic practices and disciplines. Casual sex, even between good friends, threatens to inhibit or unduly complicate the practice of faithful sex just as, in any artistic practice, it is difficult to overcome "careless" techniques learned early in one's career.

One does not need to be an artist or art critic to know how this reality works. Mistype a word once, and of course you are apt to keep mistyping it that way for the rest of the day. In the era before spell-checkers, I copied the list of words I persistently misspelled onto the inside cover of the dictionary I still keep next to my keyboard: I gave up hope of getting them straight in my mind. It's and its; to, too, two; that and which: Get them confused for too long early in life, and you will be doomed to keeping them taped to your monitor for the rest of your days. That's not a matter of intelligence. It's the power of embodiment, eyes and fingers together establishing neuron pathways.

As recent reports about the brain document, we are all the creatures of past experience, the more powerfully so in the less conscious and more highly embodied aspects of our lives.[1] Erotic responsiveness is extraordinarily complex and subtle, so we are wise indeed to approach its depths with great care for what we understand to be its ultimate significance in our lives. To the extent that sexual fidelity is understood to be a central virtue, casual sex of any kind is, at the very least, an unwise risk. Plenty of folks come through apparently unscathed, I realize. But I still think it is a significant risk, particularly for people who might be sexually active for ten or fifteen years prior to marriage. For a vocalist or a violinist, that much "bad practice" would be devastating.

We teach our kids to be honest in all things, even in small things, because life's most important moments of costly integrity depend upon exactly the same consistent spiritual discipline and practice across time. We correct their lapses not in high moral outrage but with the quiet persistence of piano teachers reproving a stiff flat finger or baseball coaches correcting batting stance: "Not like that, like this." *Here's how,* taught with care and learned with care, involves the transmission of many "habits" whose meaning and value become clear only after a long time. People achieve full or mature integrity only by internalizing it so that they know for themselves and in themselves exactly what is at stake in any particular situation they face as adults. The same is true of sexual fidelity: It can't be reduced to a simple list of "do" and "don't" that will obviate the need to develop mature judgment and self-knowledge. The best guide to sexual fidelity is a life of fidelity—to self and to other—in all of our social encounters.

Defining Marriage

I have said that serious sex is among the most vital foundations of our capacity for rich and creative relationships with other people. Let's go back to that idea. What is so vital here? Sexual intercourse, I am claiming, ought to be the exclusive and embodied language of commitment between two people. Traditionally, that sort of commitment is called "matrimony." Individual relationships of this kind are called "marriages" for heterosexuals and "domestic partnerships" for homosexuals, although that usage seems to be changing. Over the past thirty years, increasing numbers of straight couples especially among retired folks and young professionals—have lived together in seriously committed relationships but wanted to avoid the massive legal and financial implications of contractual marriage. Some gay couples, meanwhile, have sought the protections and the provisions that the legal contract offers. I need to set aside the contractual issues; I don't know enough about the legal and financial implications to have a credible opinion.[2]

Furthermore, my interest is not in the law but in the human relationship of serious, committed sexual fidelity, a relationship that I mostly refer to as "marriage." Marriage, I propose, is an alliance for its own sake and not for some good or goal or project extrinsic to the relationship itself.[3] It is not matrimony if someone marries *in order to* have children, *in order to* enjoy greater economic security or benefits, *in order to* earn society's approval, *in order to* have a noninfectious or socially sanctioned outlet for sexual desire. In matrimony, two lives are lived together for the sake of being lived together; two lives are shared for the sake of the sharing.

All sorts of other goods may follow of their own accord. They probably will, in fact. But all sorts of increased sufferings will also follow of their own accord. As Sir Francis Bacon wryly observed, he who marries yields hostages to fortune.[4] Lives that are shared are lives at risk both for each other's joy and for each other's pain. We marry "for better for worse, for richer for poorer, in sickness and in health" and not as a prudent investment.[5] In this time of AIDS, gay couples have heroically demonstrated what matrimonial fidelity can entail. Whether or not you have watched a couple struggle to the end with AIDS, surely everyone has at one time or another seen a married couple steadfastly endure through the catastrophic illness of one partner. Such duress makes public and easily visible the lineaments of fidelity that are so seldom otherwise evident.

Most teenagers do not realize just how hard life really is for most people most of the time, an innocent but implacable oblivion around which we have to navigate in talking to them about matrimony and sexual ethics. It doesn't help, in this difficult process, that most of us are also disinclined to think seriously about the suffering around us all the time. We just cope as best we can: "Sufficient unto the day is the evil thereof."[6] But for a moment here we need to consider the sad fact that life is reliably difficult for every one of us. That difficulty makes marriage an imprudent undertaking, at least if you are calculating a cost-benefit bottom line for yourself. Maybe that's why most of us marry young, while we are still unconsciously certain of our own omnipotence and invulnerability. But if matrimony is not merely a cost-benefit gamble, then what is it? It took me a very long time to realize that I did not know, or at least to realize how imprudent matrimony is and how amazingly complicated as well.

When I married Warren, a year after we graduated from the university we had both attended, getting married seemed quite conventional. A white dress, a church, an obsequious caterer—all of that. Bastille Day 1973 was the hottest, muggiest day Chicago knows how to provide. My hair curled so intensely it almost worked free of my head altogether; the veil perched atop this unruly mop like something borrowed from Charlie Chaplin. I had bought my dress in February, when the temperature was well below zero and I was recovering from the flu: It had a high neck and long sleeves. It was a beautiful dress—for February. In mid-July I clutched the prie-dieu in a stifling church and repeated after myself, "Thou shalt not faint; thou shalt not faint." I didn't faint, but I did hear the mutterings of some still, small voice arguing that here was proof positive that I had no idea what I was doing. I didn't want to listen. I pitched the veil into the back seat of my father's Ford, and we took damp but grateful refuge in the air-conditioned restaurant where luncheon was served.

Six years later, also in July, our friend Helen came for a weekend visit; by the time she left, that little voice was sounding a lot more clearly in my ears. Helen is tall but delicate, with long, graceful hands and pale blue eyes. On yet another stifling Saturday afternoon, Helen and I strolled for a couple of miles along the Lake Michigan shoreline parks in Evanston. She was thinking about marrying the fellow she had been dating, and she had come for the weekend to ask the kinds of questions old friends can ask one another. How had I come to the decision to marry Warren?

Helen had a list of questions, in fact, and as we walked along, the conversation began to feel a lot like oral comprehensive exams. Had I considered his attitude toward money? Toward children? Toward his career? Toward mine? Toward my family? Had I considered his family? Their demands on him? Their expectations of me? What about his parents' marriage? Were there dysfunctional households anywhere in his family? Inheritable diseases? Did I consider the fact that we both have asthma? Myopia? Did I consider whether we like the same weather, the same geography, the same kinds of vacations? Did I consider his taste in music? In clothes? In cooking? What about ethnic restaurants? Did my family meet his family prior to the engagement, and if so, had I taken into consideration the success of that event? Did his mother expect me to learn her Polish cooking? Did my crazy Irish clan know what to make of Warren's quiet, reserved demeanor?

They seemed like such reasonable questions, such prudent questions. I felt like an idiot. As we sat together on a park bench, Helen rolled her eyes to the sky and gestured upward in frustrated orison to whatever benevolent angel supervises ditsy women like me. Then she folded her arms and stared at me, every inch the young Harvard professor. I gulped and tried again. I had various observations on these topics, I proposed. I had some great stories. Would stories do?

No. Helen wanted to know whether and how I had done something like premarital calculations on an imaginary psychosocial spreadsheet. She was trying to construct something like a Consumer's Guide to Husbands for herself.[7] "Does Laundry: +2 (much better than average); Snores During Ragweed Season: −1 (somewhat worse than average)." By the time we got home again, back to our apartment high in an old brownstone, we had fallen silent. Helen kept glancing down at me with a distinctly worried look.

When Warren and I went to bed that night, I told him about the conversation that afternoon. He didn't have answers either.

"Did either of us think about what we were doing?" I asked. "Why did we do this?" We mulled it over for a while there in the dark, watching the curtains flap limply in the summer breeze.

"It wasn't a decision," Warren proposed at last. "Not a decision but a choice, a gut-level thing. It's not a *conclusion;* she's thinking too much. It's just something you do, something a lot bigger than thinking." I tried that out on Helen the next morning, but she was clearly skeptical.

"Did you think about whether he was thinking about it carefully enough?" she wanted to know. "Did you think he knew what he was getting into?"

Of course he didn't. And neither did I. No one can, no matter how detailed the premarital analysis: Marriage is always a leap of faith. It is far more than a merely intelligent decision: It is a voyage outward upon the deepest mysteries and paradoxes of the human condition.

Individualism and the Need for Fidelity

To an individualist like Helen, marriage is part of the larger project of self-affirmation: In matrimony, two individuals pursue their individual goals in some weakly defined federation of sovereign entities, a federation held together essentially by the goods each can supply the other, such as social propriety, sexual access, companionship, and so forth. We are in fact islands, individualism claims, but we can build bridges and maybe even breakwaters to protect both of us from the battering of a highly competitive society. "Courtship," from this perspective, becomes the consumerist scrutiny that Helen was hoping we could help her conduct thoroughly. If you are an individualist as smart, as careful, and as analytically trained as Helen, marriage looks like a speculative gamble. The young bed and wed blithely, but by age thirty or so marriage begins to look like cowboy-style venture capitalism using one's own deepest emotional reserves—and in an unregulated market besides, where everyone is looking out only for himself. "All's fair in love and war," we say. And some marriages end in the emotional equivalent of nuclear holocaust.

But I am convinced that there is something historically naive and psychologically simpleminded about the notion that a good life is one in which the individual achieves the fullest possible measure of self-esteem or self-investment in whatever values and ideas he or she has selected. I think it is shallow to suppose that the end or purpose of life is the highest possible degree of self-affirmation and self-realization. Ancient wisdom from all over the planet argues that self-absorption is a trap and not a liberation. There is something like a global moral consensus that there is more to life than me, myself, and I; there is more to you than what you can do for me. Learning how to live wisely, these spiritual disciplines insist, is something like a craft in which we spend most of our lives as apprentices "studying" with the "wise ones" of our own particular heritage and community.

Real intimacy, as I am defining it, confronts and discredits the radical individualism of our times by demonstrating the profound importance of human relationships. Just as new life depends upon and arises from sexual union, so the new growth that marks a living personality depends upon discoveries that can only happen within some level of intimate relationship, whether between matrimonial partners or between those dearest of friends who so nearly approximate mates. Without the clean and honest mirrors of intimate friendships, we are lost in that faceless crowd of faces made to meet the faces that they meet, faces designed to remain safely, anonymously conventional. Matrimony is thus the building block of all human community because it is the paradigm of friendship in general—differing in degree but not in kind. Real matrimony, as I am defining it, confronts and refutes the commonplace individualism of our times because it models a human relationship that is not centered upon the emotional equivalent of cost-benefit investment calculations.

Although matrimonial intimacy is the paradigm of the intimacy that underlies all real community, the fact remains that marriages are different in degree from friendships. I have argued that the full measure of human intimacy is necessarily sexual because our bodies are ourselves. We must undress, both emotionally and physically, in order to satisfy our deepest needs for fullest intimacy. But that undressing entails an equally full measure of vulnerability. Thus, complete intimacy cannot develop except within the security or the confidence of a serious and permanent commitment to the relationship. That's the difference in degree between good friends and marriage partners.

In the absence of full confidence in the reliability and seriousness of the commitment between partners, both common sense and psychic self-preservation will demand a guardedness, a holding back, a tentativeness that impedes the development of full intimacy. Or so I claim. And it is a claim, a premise, upon which much of my argument depends. Furthermore, it explains a key difficulty in talking to our kids about sex: The young are, on the whole, blissfully but unconsciously certain of their own invulnerability. They do not realize—as we do—how profoundly they can be hurt by a casual sexual affair or the sexual infidelity of a spouse.

Vulnerability and Compassion

I have argued at length that the fullest or richest realization of our sexuality takes place within committed relationships. We need that security not only for our own safety but also in order for our vulnerability to become fully conscious. Only as vulnerability becomes more conscious can it develop as it ought to develop. In the secure environment offered by a mature and committed relationship, vulnerability can be transformed from a lack or a deficiency into the gift of compassion, which is to say into the strength or the wisdom to understand that our suffering need never destroy us. Were we invulnerable, we would be heartless. Were we invulnerable, we would be incapable of relationships and incapable of creativity. Only as vulnerability evolves into compassion can we face life's pain with the serenity or equanimity that is the fruit of maturity.

There are many paths to that enlightenment; marriage is only one of many. In fact, I suspect that marriage is the least recognized of these paths. As I complained before, most accounts of the spiritual journey presume that the seeker is sexually ascetic if not entirely solitary. I understand that: Although in a quiet week I can spend eight or ten hours writing, I am primarily a homemaker presiding over a houseful of cereal bowls and soccer balls, physics books and fencing gear, art projects and biology projects and the unsewn pieces of quilts. Troops of teenagers thunder in and out, all of them hungry. It's distracting all right. And there are not as many quiet weeks as I might wish for. What little solitude I can find for prayer or for writing is precious indeed. Amid this commonplace reality, amid this suburban, middle-class, Midwest existence, I have slowly realized that spiritual discipline is required for anyone to sustain the intimacy that marriage is and requires. Jon Kabat-Zinn at one point describes his own babies as little Zen masters, parachuted into his life to demonstrate to him all over again how attached he can be to his own egotistic gratification.[8] I laughed until I choked. But his wisdom has proved very helpful indeed.

Living with somebody, day in and day out, year after year after year, and especially with the added stress of childrearing, produces an incredible vulnerability between partners. That's why so many marriages fail. In a marriage, sexual union enacts and expresses that vulnerability and resolves it into some of the most powerful pleasure that life can offer anyone. Marital sex is thus a wellspring from which the roots of compassion are watered. It nourishes the creative, compassionate generativity that childrearing demands and that can be expressed in so many other ways as well. The power of sex both celebrates and strengthens the intimacy that full sexual development requires. If the spiritual journey is to be sexually realized rather than sexually ascetic, fidelity is crucial.

Acknowledging Each Other's Needs

I want to look more specifically at the vulnerabilities that couples experience within committed relationships, so as to delineate more clearly the role that fidelity plays in creating and sustaining intimacy. Fidelity is not a contract clause governing the organs of reproduction. Fidelity is not simply an agreement about sexual exclusivity. As I said in Chapter One, fidelity is intrinsic to the happiness and the life of a happy marriage. It's time to look closely at how that happens.

First of all, intimacy demands the acknowledgment of one another's needs at face value, without question. Your needs are no longer merely yours but as nearly my own as possible. If you say you need something, I need for you to have it—without second-guessing, without cautious, evaluative skepticism. That means that each must be responsible for evaluating the appropriateness of his or her own claims. A marriage is not a miniature free market in which every contender makes the largest demands that the system will tolerate. Marriage is an ethical commitment that resides within a network of ideas about right and wrong behavior.

Ethical demands—unlike wage or price demands—have internal boundaries or limits. We must be honest and mature in expressing our needs, so as to avoid both self-indulgence and injury to our spouses. And we must recognize that even legitimate needs cannot always be satisfied. Life is hard. But that is certainly not the fault of our spouses. It is not their responsibility to meet our needs but rather to live alongside us, with whatever unmet or unmeetable needs we may have. Recognizing how vulnerable each spouse is to the other, we must be cautious and mature in our demands even upon each other's empathy.

Nonetheless, there are myriad ways in which spouses can meet one another's needs, myriad generosities small and large wherein we can discover that it is in giving that we receive. For instance, I know a marriage in which she is deathly afraid of heights, probably a true acrophobic. His idea of the perfect vacation is climbing up a sheer rock face; since adolescence, he has spent a couple of weeks every summer climbing with a fellow who has been that sort of friend for decades. They literally put their lives in one another's hands. She doesn't go along to watch because she could not endure to. Home alone in Evanston, she worries. She calls me, and we go out for lemon bars and coffee.

Even in the intimacy of our old and dear friendship, she does not begrudge him the time, the expense, or the danger. He needs his rock climbing. She cannot fathom why, but she accepts that he does and makes no complaint. Thereby, as it turns out, she shares in the spiritual and emotional renewal he achieves. She shares the high, if not the heights. It is a vivid example of a reality that finds a thousand petty echoes in almost every marriage, even in something so simple as watching football on TV or belonging to a book group that reads fluffy novels.

But that kind of relaxation and renewal is just the beginning. I have another friend who has a fabulous perennial garden, including an artificial pond with water lilies. She and her husband replaced the driveway some years ago with an exotic metal gridwork through which grass can grow so that the swath of concrete would not disrupt the harmony of her yard. The only problem is that she has a bad back. When there is heavy work to be done—laying that grid, digging that pond—he does it for her under her painstaking supervision. But it's not that he too is a gardener. He is, she realizes, quite without opinions of any sort.

What he notices and cares about is her need to create beauty and to live surrounded by beauty. We sat on her porch one afternoon drinking iced tea, and I dared to ask whether she resented his oblivion to it all. She didn't. And as we talked, I realized how profoundly blessed she felt by his perception not of the landscape but of her own deeply rooted aesthetic sense. He sees and nurtures that beauty in her. His indifference to her delphiniums measures his recognition of truths about her that she needs acknowledged far more than she needs praise for her garden. The whole neighborhood is agog about that garden, after all. Its spiritual origins in a very quiet and private woman are hidden from almost everyone—but not from him. She is probably the most beautiful woman I know, but she has trouble recognizing or acknowledging her own good looks. But I see them acknowledged, plain as day, in her husband's demeanor around her. He holds a mirror up for her, a mirror that begins in his large, almost hazel brown eyes.

Truly to acknowledge the other's needs at face value, despite fear of heights or indifference to delphiniums, is to trust each other's absolute honesty and mature self-knowledge in claiming, "I need this." The potential for abuse is simply astounding, and surely many marriages come to grief upon these rocks. But that sad fact does not impinge upon the importance of what's going on when the claim is honestly made and honestly heard.

To acknowledge needs at face value can be to solace pain that lies far beyond the ordinary boundary of what can be articulated or directly revealed. Such acknowledgment nurtures those depths that remain secluded in the mystery at the heart of each of us: Visible or declared needs can be emblems or emanations of needs that are perforce invisible. Such compassion is costly stuff. It can be very painful indeed to suffer the slings and arrows of each other's outrageous fortunes, especially when as a practical matter there is nothing to do or no way to help. But for the relationship itself, it does not make a lot of difference whether or not we have the resources to solve each other's problems or to meet each other's needs. What matters is how this quality of nonjudgmental compassion helps to sustain the perception of each other as separate, distinct, ultimately unknowable others. Both partners are drawn outside of themselves as centers of cost-benefit calculation because they must learn to care for and to care about someone outside their control. A permanent, embedded, embodied responsibility for someone else can be a transforming experience. It is not to be undertaken lightly because it can be as spectacularly damaging as it can be spectacularly vital or graceful.

Trusting Each Other's Integrity

Intimacy also demands full and absolute trust in the beloved's integrity. For instance, one of my best friends is married to an engineer—an exceedingly witty and handsome fellow, in fact—whose company sometimes does highly classified consulting work on government contracts. When he travels—handcuffed to his briefcase—he cannot tell her where he is going or for how long. He cannot call her once he is there, and he cannot return from a trip early just because, for instance, a child has broken a leg or she has gone into labor to give birth.

She worries at times about coping alone, but that's about all. Trusting him is never a question. She is bothered far more, in fact, by the fact that they cannot mix socially with foreign nationals. She is not even supposed to tell such people why she is declining their invitations or failing to extend one. We live in a community of immigrants: The school district reports eighty-seven different languages as the primary speech of families. When soccer games get close, the cheering and advice erupt into a cacophony of tongues. There is something crazy-making, in her mind, about this demand that she avoid so many of the other soccer moms. She shrugs and copes as wisely as she can: His work requires this from her, and that's enough. She figures that if he can put up with her family, she can put up with his security clearance. Life just makes these demands, she says. I suspect the two of them are saints, but it is evident that their marriage is deeply contented.

Again, this is an extreme instance of a commonplace reality. Lots of folks sometimes have to work late or on weekends in ways that disrupt the routines or the expectations of their spouses. Many of us work with people whom we find sexually attractive. If nothing else, all of us are always spending shared resources on items of purely individual use or value. And all of us are always deciding whether to do chores or whether to do something we enjoy or whether we need above all to collapse in a comfortable heap and do nothing in particular. In marriage, it is vital to trust the other's integrity in making these accounts or in making these decisions because there are myriad ways in which people can exploit one another. In the early romance of a relationship it may seem not to matter who does the dishes or the laundry, who pays the bills or shops for groceries or keeps the coffee table cleared. But in time, it does matter.

Reciprocity Rather Than "Equality"

And so the third key aspect of vulnerability within intimacy is how deeply intimacy depends not upon equality but upon reciprocity. Equality can be counted out; reciprocity cannot. Equality is measurable; fidelity gives without measure. In the very early years of our marriage, friends of ours kept a checklist in the kitchen, held to the fridge by a magnet. A column on the far left listed various household chores; each was assigned points according to the time and effort involved. A row across the top listed days of the week. Each time a chore was completed, the husband or the wife would scribble an initial at the intersection of day and chore. Subtotals were calculated both weekly and monthly, and their goal was to achieve essentially identical totals at least monthly, if not weekly. The objective rationality of the scheme had some modest appeal, I admit, as we wrangled back and forth with our own version of the Housework Wars.

But since then I've realized that life does not yield itself to objective and rational schemes. Life is just too complex. Totting up points on a grid cannot tell the truth that must be known or guard the values that must be preserved. "For better for worse" ebbs and flows far more often and far less predictably than charts allow; nor are there points that tell the value of Warren's bringing me coffee in the morning or my turning on his side of the electric blanket to warm the bed when he is working late at his desk.

If you are adding up points, such small acts appear to cancel each other out. If you are building an intimate relationship, such small acts of kindness are valuable beyond measure. If you are adding up points, you have an eye on the running total. If you are building an intimate relationship, you have an eye on the person you love and the whole life that you share. I have come to think of this deeper reality as "the one-life clause." It's a domestic version of "From each according to his ability; to each according to his needs." Needs and abilities fluctuate with time and circumstance, but if there is one life, then there is one bottom line rather than competing totals.

It remains crucial to recognize how easily and how profoundly we fall into exploiting one another. Money, housework, emotional support, childcare, in-laws, career demands: Such issues are part and parcel of sexual ethics because these are among the ordinary sources of vulnerability to each other's greed, laziness, ambition, egotism, and so forth. Trusting each other's integrity demonstrates that marriage is not a mechanical or arithmetical quid-pro-quo arrangement but rather the gutsiest, most nitty-gritty test of what it means to have faith in another person. If my accountability is to the chart on the fridge and not to you, then I can do what totals to "my half" and then go read a novel—no matter what your needs may be. Or if I'm locked in battle with a stubborn, inarticulate manuscript and my score starts to fall, then I'm "one down" in my relationship with you. Anger, guilt, and frustration start to feed one another. But in a genuinely intimate relationship, my accountability is to myself and to you and not to some ratings chart. Life's external demands do not get any easier, but at least the marriage doesn't serve to amplify the problems.

In marriage, each partner faces the challenge of knowing the self and knowing the spouse, knowing the self's needs and limitations and knowing those of the spouse. Each is challenged to grow up. Partners must renounce both pseudo-saintly claims to martyrdom and pseudoheroic claims to invulnerable strength. The manipulative powers of dominance and guilt must be set aside and kept aside.

When both partners are fully and honestly attentive both to self and to other in this way, then the potential for exploitation falls dramatically because the efforts of each person are not only mutually perceived but mutually experienced. Compassion grows into the space created by the thousand small habits and routine practices that over time build up the reality of faithfulness. The self-abandonment or openness or vulnerability of the sexual act either enacts the fundamental quest for fully reciprocal fidelity in the relationship or enacts an exchange that is governed like an investment and is inherently exploitative in its primary focus on the self as a center of cost-benefit calculation. The structural or inherent reciprocity of erotic desire sacramentally and physically enacts the material reciprocity of two lives lived and shared as one life. One's arousal is part of the other's arousal just as one's "terrible, horrible, no-good, very bad week" is part of the other's week.

In short, there's nothing wrong with lists of things to do on the fridge. Every household needs them. But a scorecard is not OK. The several marriages I knew that used scorecards did not last very long, and I've come to recognize the score-card mentality as a sign that a relationship is deteriorating. Successful marriages, on the other hand, seem often to involve the risky generosity that gives without counting cost or calculating merit. The commitment of full sexual fidelity creates a secure inner landscape in which to live out that adventure in all its improbable risk. That's why sexual fidelity is the material or bodily enactment of a commitment that is of the whole person—not merely something cerebral or merely a contract delineating exclusive rights to the organs of reproduction.

Mutual Care

Intimacy creates, depends upon, and ultimately transforms vulnerability because marriage demands a full mutuality of attention and energy, each for the other. Marriage is not simply an idea, nor is it merely a set of feelings. It is more than an ability to communicate, just as it must be more than a house kept in common or children jointly nurtured. As life lived in common, as lives shared for the sake of the sharing, marriage depends upon material or literal participation in the realities of one another's lives. And so fidelity is neither a contract nor an attitude but a set of practices or habits—disciplines, in the old sense—whereby two lives are lived in gracious accord with one another. This notion is an elusive reality that Warren and I have lived our way into gradually, not quite knowing what we were about or why. We did it because we were told to.

About six or seven weeks after our first child was born, late in my maternity leave, I went up to the library one afternoon to attend a guest lecture on illustrations of Goethe's *Faust.* It was a gorgeous day in early March: cold, clear, sunny, with almost a hint of a promise of warmth in the sun. The walk up to campus felt wonderful, even though the sidewalks were lumpy with old snow. It was probably the first real exercise I had had in months, and I was feeling vibrantly, incredibly, gloriously alive. The lecture was interesting and well attended, and—best of all—for a solid hour I could sit quietly without liability to the unpredictable demands of a newborn. I enjoyed myself thoroughly.

Afterward I left the small lecture hall with a fellow from the school of music, speaking softly and walking quietly through the towering ranges of books in the library. He congratulated me on my new baby and asked the usual new-baby questions. Suddenly he stopped walking, so I stopped too. In just a couple of steps, he backed me more or less out of sight into the empty space between a structural pillar and the end of a range. He put down his briefcase so he could gesture with both hands, as if he were conducting an invisible orchestra.

"Look," he said, his German accent thickening abruptly. "You don't know what you are doing, you two. You think you know, but you don't. You want babies, and you want this too?" He gestured down the long rows of library books. I could almost hear a crescendo of my own professional ambitions.

And he went on to tell me that all his friends were getting divorced—the agonized sundering of lives that had been shared for decades. At some point, he promised, our new baby and any others we had would all be grown. Or if not grown, at least gone. Summer camp. College. Then, for the first time in maybe twenty years, the parents are alone. The parents for the first time in so many years have a chance to talk without interruption. And then what? Then there is nothing to say. After so long a silence, after so many years of attention only to work and to household and to children, there is nothing left between them to say. They are strangers. Strangers!

I looked up at him, bewildered. He was a stranger too. I hardly knew him. He was very handsome, with chiseled features and a powerfully aristocratic manner made all the more elegant by how dramatically his hair was streaked with gray at the temples. But he was decades older than I was. I had only spoken to him a couple of times before. One of his freshmen had enrolled in a writing course I was teaching, and he had kept a close and fatherly eye on the boy's progress. But we had never spoken again—at the time, I did not even know what department he was in. What was going on?

Then he told me about how he and his wife had fled Nazi Germany in the late '30s, about how both of them had lost to the death camps all the family they left behind, about how they had felt besieged and isolated by both anti-Semitism and anti-German sentiment in America in the '40s. All this added up to feeling desperate to sustain their own marriage so as to sustain and eventually re-create the familial heritage destroyed but for them. They were such a tiny remnant of so many dead.

As I listened, I was at first startled to see that their commitment to each other was for him transparently synonymous with their commitment to their children. All those relationships had seemed threatened by the world around them in the 1940s and '50s. In a world that cannot be trusted, in a world of such bad faith, he felt that his marriage offered to his children the crucial example of what real fidelity means and how real fidelity both exists and can be trusted. And now, in the 1970s, he felt that fragile heritage of fidelity threatened again by the rising tide of midlife divorce.

"Do this," he said to me suddenly, taking a deep breath and pulling himself up in full professorial decorum. "Do this: Every week, every week no matter what, go out one evening together. Dinner. We, we never become strangers. Once a week, always. Do this. Both of you scholars, and babies too? Make time before it is too late, before there is no time left." His voice wavered slightly; he fell silent and looked away. We stood a while in the privacy of two long rows of books. Then I bowed and thanked him, and we walked in silence the rest of the way out of the library.

We do it. We do it, and we remember him, although I never had a chance to tell him that we had taken his advice to heart. And besides, "advice" seems too tame a word for that conversation. But it is a story I have told over and over through the years, always to someone astounded and indeed envious that Warren and I have always made this kind of time for one another. It is clearly not a common habit: Especially once there are children, spouses seem all too seldom to make time to do things alone together—except, I suppose, making love. But that should not be the only time the couple is alone, awake, and exclusively attentive to one another.

There is nothing magic about going out to dinner, of course. Nor have we always done it that way. When we have not had enough money to eat out, we have gone for long drives or walks. Nor are these evenings primarily a chance for conversation. Often we are too tired for much talk; often we have eaten or walked mostly in companionable silence, in comfortable solace from the verbal performances of the day. Even when it happens, the talk mostly resembles the desultory chat of old friends catching up with one another.

Our time together is valuable not as a forum for something else but as an invaluable respite from all of life's implacable demands. It is an enduring testimony that each matters to the other enough to set aside regular time from life's responsibilities simply to be together without any agenda at all. In marriage as in any other relationship, the deepest sorts of conversation happen when and as they will and not, therefore, in any predictable way on our Wednesday nights out. Wednesday nights are merely the common foundation upon which we assemble the week's collage of issues and ideas and decisions— all the small bits of conversation that happen en route to the train or while doing dishes. Furthermore, the habit insists to the children that the core of this family is the marriage of the parents and not the children themselves—and certainly not that list of things to do held to the fridge by a magnet. A couple of times we let the habit lapse, and we found that our life together grew progressively, inexplicably more difficult.

My best explanation for our Wednesdays, even after so many years, is a metaphor. Certain kinds of trees will be shaped in their growth by the impinging presence of other plants. Out my study window I can see a mature honey locust with a curve in the north side of its crown where a Chinese elm used to fit. The elm had sprouted too close to the foundation of the garage, and when we first bought this house we chopped it down. That was almost ten years ago, but the locust has not grown into that empty curve. Time together without an agenda or desultory, aimless, attentive conversation in which anything might surface, places exactly that sort of pressure upon the growth of the individual spouses.

Wednesday nights are not a chance to say, "You forgot to enter a check in the register," or "I'll be in Cleveland the weekend of the seventeenth," or "I think there's trouble with the transmission in the washing machine." Wednesday nights are not an exercise in five-minute management. They are just a chance to lean on one another, in many senses of that word. We cast shadows and twine roots and provide some measure of shelter from the wind. Our time alone together is as vital as our individual time entirely alone. Psychologists of course attribute considerable power and importance to what surfaces in such "agendaless" time, but whether or not psychodynamics explains all of it, such times do render us permanently vulnerable to one another in the shape and direction of our individual growth, just as the tree outside my study demonstrates. As the years tick past, that vulnerability has become stunningly evident to me.

As my music school colleague claimed, this time together is crucial. But that very centrality makes it dangerous as well, and the danger demonstrates the need for integrity and commitment to the relationship. Sexual fidelity is the physical enactment of the encompassing fidelity that reaches deep into the depths of all that we are. Remember Faust: We trade our souls or we take our chances. There's really no alternative. A sexual relationship in which bets are hedged may not dissolve into angry divorce, but neither will it achieve real matrimony.

Psychic Boundaries: Neither Lost nor Armed

Such a depth of intimacy, such a permanent, embedded, embodied vulnerability to another is nonetheless quite difficult: No marriage achieves perfect acceptance of needs, perfect integrity and trust, perfectly reciprocal responsibility, and perfectly sustained mutual care. All such virtues are always on the edge: They are governing ideals, not concrete realities like sidewalks marching around a house. Furthermore, the ongoing struggle toward such intimacy challenges and deepens the psychological boundaries between the partners. The paradox here is both profound and massive. Intimacy is lost if the two literally become one, if the psychological boundaries between them dissolve. Under the pressure of real intimacy, each becomes clearer about what those boundaries are, where they are, and why they are vital. But intimacy is also lost if the boundaries are armed, if one or both partners must remain on guard against the other's judgmentalism or indifference.

The difficulty of maintaining appropriate boundaries can be estimated from the vehemence with which both men and women have denounced marriage as both corrupt and corrupting. Men feel absorbed and exploited for their economic and emotional capacity to provide. Women feel absorbed and exploited for their physical and emotional capacity to care. Both husbands and wives can feel lost, annihilated, consumed; each can unequivocally—and unself-consciously— blame the other or, at best, a concretized abstraction called the "institution" of marriage.

As I said before, granting a marriage license to an exploitative relationship does not make that relationship either moral or mature. But there is a deeper reality at work in these complaints. Both having sex and living together inevitably blur the boundaries between two people, with all the temptations to denial and to projection that such blurring invites. There is one bed, one bathroom sink, one dinner table, and one supply of daily newspapers. And so there is great temptation for partners to blame one another for their own confusions, uncertainty, or inability to be honest. But these are failures of mature self-knowledge, not flaws in marriage as such. If a person is centrally uncertain about his or her own identity, then marriage will prove hazardous indeed.

Gaining intimacy with another person—a relationship in which boundaries are neither lost nor armed—is a lot like learning to play the violin or the trombone or any other instrument in which there is no simple, precise mechanical aid to the physical location of notes, as there is, for instance, on the piano. At first, the variety of sour screeches can seem infinite. But that does not mean that the instrument itself is incapable of great music. True performance is merely difficult. It takes practice. It requires both instruction and role models. Above all, it takes persistence, humility, forgiveness, and a sense of humor.

Marital intimacy does not and cannot entail oblivion to one another's failures and problems. Somehow or other—there is no easy way to explain how—the partners accept one another's faults. All human characters have faults. We all have blind spots, and we all have difficult needs. The progressive self-revelation of marriage involves a progressive acceptance both of self and of other. Each learns to accept and to cope with the other's faults as part of the unfortunate givens of adult life, something like head colds or dark winter mornings or taxes. The other's faults become a lot like bad weeks at work or troublesome relatives: just part of the shared trouble of a shared life. Both partners know what the problems are; both do their best to live with them in a spirit of mature humility and generous faith that each is honestly endeavoring to become the finest person possible. More powerfully yet, each learns what it feels like to be loved and accepted not in denial of but rather in despite of one's own faults. And that acceptance is an extraordinary experience. I can imagine no greater empowering impetus to repentance and reform.

This quality of mature and insightful acceptance is what distinguishes matrimony as I envision it from the marketplace alliances of individualism, no matter how strictly the contract demands sexual exclusivity. What I am talking about goes far beyond Barney's song, "I Love You." The deepest intimacy is not quid pro quo. The deepest intimacy rests not upon the effort to love you as you love me and vice versa but rather upon the effort to love unconditionally, to love with the depth and the maturity that the word "fidelity" names most accurately. Such love is a fine and delicate achievement. I think it is so hard to do that the vast majority of people need the assurance and the support of committed and faithful embodied relationships even to begin to try. There are saints among us, of course, who can love like this singlehandedly and without having that love returned. But for most of us, most of the time, even ordinary marriage is no easy task.

I cannot objectively account for how people can change and grow quite profoundly while yet remaining in a marriage that grows and changes right alongside. I don't think it can be attributed in any simple way to skill or maturity or any merely personal quality. If I have to name a "causal" agent, I'm inclined to call it *grace.* That is, we are indeed loved unconditionally by God. Because we are created in God's image and sustained by the energy of God's love, we can—with real effort and with real skill—attain some small measure of the same unconditional and enduring love in our own relationships.

Fidelity, Intimacy, and Community

Nonetheless, marriages depend vitally upon the sustenance of a community. It is terribly difficult to sustain matrimonial intimacy if every other aspect of life requires
relentless vigilance against exploitation, neglect, and abuse.
The breakdown of matrimony in our society probably
reflects the simultaneous breakdown of community as a primary nurturant and supportive structure in everyone's life.

Radical individualism in America posits a profound
dichotomy between trusting private life and ruthless public
behavior, but to do so is to ignore the fact that open vulnerability is a delicate achievement. No one can erect and shed
emotional defenses with the ease of changing hats. Furthermore, willing vulnerability and full maturity are reciprocal
achievements: Full maturity will develop slowly if at all
when most of life takes place within that matrix of bickering
and brutality that so commonly characterizes public life. In
short—and again, as I was cautioned—our fidelity to our
spouses is directly threatened by a society of bad faith.

Ideally, marriages are situated within and supported by
communities of belief that articulate, over and over again, the
unfailing faithfulness of the Holy, by whatever name the Holy
is known, communities of belief whose members struggle in
every real way to keep faith with one another. At least theo-
retically or theologically, Christian churches are among the
loci for such communities. As William Willimon argues,

> Not having sex with other people's spouses, for instance, is
> for us a political act, a claim about what God means for
> humanity, our way of witnessing to a God who is faithful
> and requires us to be so. Christians are required to chal-
> lenge a culture in which everyone is a commodity, by

demonstrating relations with one another based not on use but on love. We are able to do so because that is the way God has dealt with us. Our politics . . . is aligned with our worship. Any discussion about ethics, whether of the bedroom or of the boardroom, is for us preceded by the question, Well, which God do you worship?[9]

Dante observes that the leader is one who sees the towers of the True City—but not necessarily the easiest way through the intervening woods. "How to get there" is always worked out ad-lib. Despite their failures, communities of belief and spiritual practice see those towers to the extent that they attest to the abiding reality of what cannot be explained or understood. They can help us remain open to how much in our own lives cannot be explained or understood but only enacted.

Life is very hard, after all, and wisdom is costly stuff. True discernment is a rare gift and a fragile heritage. It's not something that can be easily institutionalized, written up into bylaws, or managed by attorneys and accountants and governing committees. I am beginning to suspect that churches, synagogues, and the like are merely places where, from time to time, communities sprout like colonies of wildflowers in the woods, like the gloriosa daisies from a decade ago that still sprout with all the passion of van Gogh in unexpected places in the yard.

Community does something else as well, something other than attesting to the elusive depths of life. Community is also a place where friendships can blossom. As a variety of friendship, every marriage vitally depends upon the spouses having important friendships outside the marriage itself. Each spouse can more easily grow and subsist within the marriage if that marital relationship is merely the deepest and not the exclusive form of intimacy that life offers.

Any spouse has interests that the other spouse does not share, mundane needs that the other spouse cannot satisfy. To suppose that marriage can supply all such needs borders upon viewing matrimony as psychic fusion, and to ignore the nurture and the vitality of friendships borders upon willful stupidity. A great many people especially in our time live deeply satisfying and productive lives without spouses. They have friends, and they are friends. They offer absolutely crucial public witness to how rich friendship can be and to how profoundly we are called to be friends at that level. They defy pernicious aspects of the radical division between private behavior and public behavior.

Parents' friends are also central to the process of teaching sexual ethics to children and to adolescents, because they are role models for how friends behave. Kids should abstain from sex, but even toddlers have friends. At an early age, kids set about acquiring friends and learning how to be friends: What every four-year-old most earnestly desires is a chauffeur and a social secretary. But they need much more than such functionaries might provide. They need help in learning about friendship. We are teaching the foundation of sexual ethics every time we talk to kids about kindness, honesty, or responsibility in these young friendships. We are laying the foundation of sexual ethics when we teach our kids not to exploit one another, not to be cruel, not to be manipulative. It's a long, slow process: We may be taught everything we need to know in kindergarten, but it is a life's work to learn those lessons thoroughly.

Many kids are terribly cruel, and I think most kids are oblivious to the kindness of their friends until they have been hurt deeply enough and often enough by the poorly socialized among their peers. Amidst the long and soul-consuming process of teaching our three about friendship, I have been grateful beyond words for examples from my friends of how friends ought to behave. A sympathetic phone call, advice on hanging wallpaper, the loan of a car. Anything, everything, can be a chance to name and to teach the reality of friendship as a concrete, embodied, enacted bond and not merely a set of sentiments. Kids who have learned not to exploit one another over access to computer games will quickly enough recognize the temptation to exploit or to tolerate exploitation over access to one another's bodies.

From classical antiquity onward, teaching and learning about friendship and about hospitality has been understood in the West as the foundation of practical instruction in ethics. When marriage was regarded primarily as a dynastic and economic contract, the governing model of sexual ethics was property rights. But if we regard matrimony primarily as a sexually enacted friendship, then we can call into relevance a rich and fascinating history of inquiry into the character of friendship and hospitality. Better yet, we can relax a little and realize that in large measure we know what we are doing, and we have been doing it all along with our kids.

Nonetheless, we need friends to hold up to our kids as models, and we need them to become the adult friends of our kids. We can't do it alone. Two good parents are not enough, because in most circumstances children are willfully oblivious to the relationship between their own parents. For kids, parents are *parents*: a sexless, alien, protohominid species peculiarly concerned with hygiene and homework and courtesy. But children are close observers and ferocious mimics of the style and content of parents' friendships.

We need friends and we need community, because the integrity upon which intimacy depends stands so close to the deepest mysteries of what it is to be human. Evil needs no such support, after all. No one doubts the possibility of evil.

Virtue is what's mysterious, and to face the mysterious we always need the company of friends. I had an amazing glimpse of that loneliness one spring almost twenty years ago. At the time, I was teaching Milton's *Paradise Lost* as part of a "great books" course. One bright Tuesday morning, one of my students walked through the open door of my office, flung herself into the chair by my desk, and burst into tears. I started and set down my red pen. Now what?

On Monday we had discussed the section in *Paradise Lost* where Milton describes the delights of conjugal sexuality before the Fall. "Imparadis't in one another's arms," Adam and Eve enjoy "thir fill / Of bliss on bliss" (IV:506–508).[10] In their Bower of Bliss,

> Here Love his golden shafts imploys, here lights
> His constant Lamp, and waves his purple wings,
> Reigns here and revels. (IV:763–765)

Milton's description of their sexual delight rapidly builds to as vivid a rendering as anything I have ever read or seen at the movies.

After the Fall, their sensual delight gives way to a brutal, egotistical lust: The forbidden fruit gets them drunk, and they fall into bed for as degrading a scene of drunken sex as Hollywood has ever produced. They wake up with a truly epic hangover and a vindictive loathing of one another. I thought that Monday's class had kept its balance between the extremes of prudery and vulgarity in working through the scenes, although many students had been—as always—just a bit nonplussed by the vivid presence of the erotic in a banal university classroom. I was only in my late twenties, but I was ex officio a grownup even if not a parent—and therefore presumed to be entirely clueless about the erotic. Students had been, as usual, transparently astounded that an English professor not only understood the erotic passages but could talk about their presence in the text with unembarrassed facility and objectivity. The memory of Monday's discussion erupted in my mind like an unexpected flashbulb: Had something upset this kid? Milton outrages plenty of people, after all, for very good reasons and in several different ways.

I put aside the paper I was grading and pulled a box of tissues from a desk drawer. I turned toward her slightly, sat back in my finest imitation of professional composure, and waited for her to speak. It took her a few minutes to collect herself and find her voice, by which time I could feel mine starting to strangle in my throat. It was a very big class. I recognized her face—she was tall and remarkably beautiful, she always sat third from the front in the last row by the windows, and she always laughed at my jokes. But her name? I had no idea. I hoped one of Milton's angels was watching over me.

After several tissues, she explained that in reading Milton she finally understood why she had resisted the overwhelming social pressure to hop into bed with every single guy she dated more than once. Those who were still virgins by the high school senior prom, she said, were considered hopelessly weird—repressed or Puritanical or frigid. And here she was, a college sophomore and still a virgin. She knew there had to be more to sex than that, she sobbed, and Milton said it for her; Milton knew. She wasn't weird. She was right!

She had called home the night before to try to tell her mother what she had just told me. But when she tried to read the poetry to her mother, she just cried so hard she couldn't keep reading. Her mother told her to come talk to me, so here she was. I felt dwarfed and astounded by the trust that advice implied. That unknown woman had put her daughter's heart in my hands.

As this student recounted so eloquently, the pressure to have sex can be enormous. It's not simply that healthy, happy young people have sexual drives as strong and as vital as everything else about them. Heaven knows that's real enough, all by itself. The demands of education in our society commonly delay marriage for years and years after the dawn of sexual maturity. Abstinence can be excruciating. But the most difficult pressure to have sex is not biological drives but cultural demands, which include this assumption that abstinence shows emotional immaturity or repression, that abstinence signals impotence or frigidity, that there is no intelligent and constructive reason to treat sexuality as anything more than a simple physical appetite like the need for food and water.

On the contrary, as I have argued, the complex reciprocity of sexual desire both enacts and presupposes the full and mature intimacy that can grow only within a faithful and committed relationship. This undergraduate had learned the value of sexual fidelity from her parents. She had learned it clearly enough to withstand what had turned into years of extremely painful peer pressure that was progressively eroding her own sexual confidence. What mattered to her, what brought her to tears and then—with some prompting—to my office was her hope and her terrible relief at finding external support for what her parents had taught and how her parents had lived. Milton's sensual skill with words, no less than his thunderous claim to be the compeer of scriptural poets, convinced her that she was not alone. We all need that kind of company to sustain our commitment to commitment, our fidelity to the very idea of fidelity—Milton no less than everyone else. He prays at one point that an angel of the Lord will for his poem "fit audience find, though few" (VII:31).

That Tuesday Milton had his audience, right there in my office clutching blue tissue. I had several subsequent conversations with that young woman, and then with at least four or five others as word got around: It was a three-box term for my tissue supply. I was overwhelmed by the pain and confusion in the lives of these absolutely decent and marvelous young people—who are now, of course, close to forty years old themselves and for all I know themselves the mothers of teenagers.

In these conversations, I was dismayed by the profound irrelevance of my philosophic training and my not inconsiderable supply of systematic theological ideas and doctrines and beliefs. I didn't believe in God at that point, but after sixteen years of Catholic education and a lot of work on Coleridge's theology, I could talk the talk quite fluently. But these women didn't want elaborate deductions from first principles in theology or ontology. They wanted moral support from me in resisting what they experienced as sexual exploitation enforced by broad and powerful threats of social ostracism. Above all, they wanted my story. They wanted to know if I was faithful and why and what that meant to me and whether I knew other good-looking young women who were as weird as I was. Above all they wanted to know why—given easy access to good birth control and abortion—why we confronted the status quo in these costly ways. What is it about sex? Why not do it just for fun?

I couldn't say. I didn't know. I started having dreams in which I was walled in by boxes of blue tissue, from which prison I could escape only by knowing what to say—but I didn't know what to say. I could say only that I had been abstinent from sheer terror of Irish fertility and then discovered that by happenstance my husband and I were developing something that was well en route to a power and a significance I had no idea how to name. I would shrug and smile, feeling myself do that just as my father once did.

They were content. They didn't need argument, I suppose, but the clarity and passion of my testimony. I might have quoted Hamlet, a line I often used to escape when the transcendent threatened to intrude: "There are more things in heaven and earth, Horatio, / than are dreamt of in your philosophy" (I:v). But my inability to account for my life burned the question deep in my soul, far deeper than I heeded at the time, a depth I rediscovered when I found myself still so inarticulate in front of my son.

At the time I was mostly aware of that other mom: her trust, her gutsy recognition that none of us can do this alone. We are not islands, separate from the main, but an elusive, ineffable unity that we can glimpse in the best and rarest of moments.

Talking to Kids About Intimacy

At least in the late '60s, to ask, "Are they intimate?" was to ask, "Are they having intercourse?" To be intimate was to have sex: That's what the word meant. The word "intimate" still floats around as shorthand for "sexually intimate," which is a euphemism of sorts for any mutual sexual activity culminating in orgasm.

But that's a collapse in the meaning of a word with a rich and interesting history of its own—a history that, as Samuel Taylor Coleridge was so fond of observing, encodes the history of culture itself. As a scholarly Coleridgean (once upon a time), I have immediate recourse in any complicated discussion with our three children when asked what exactly a word really means. We keep the compact *Oxford English Dictionary* in its slipcase on the hearth and a big, thumb-notched *American Heritage Dictionary* under the coffee table. At least in this house, it's a useful strategy—and they have not yet asked me to hide that big dictionary when their friends are coming over.

"Intimacy" is from the Latin adjective *intimus,* which means *inmost* or *deepest.* That's a fine place to start: Truly intimate relationships are the deepest ones, the ones that involve our innermost realities. But that's not all there is to the word. Our adjective "intimate" doesn't just mean "private" or "closed off from the outside." Quite the contrary, in fact, as its etymology attests. That Latin adjective *intimus* gave rise to a late Latin verb, *intimare,* a verb that means "to put or bring in" or "to publish or announce." Intimacy happens, etymologically speaking, when the inmost depth is opened to what another may bring in. Intimacy happens when the inmost depth is revealed or announced to another. The English verb "to intimate" means something like "to hint" or "to suggest"—gentle actions, gentle speech suitable to relationships on that innermost terrain. "Illicit sexual intercourse" shows up literally in last place in the *American Heritage* list of definitions of the noun "intimacy."

The linguistic history of "intimacy" mirrors our increasing cultural difficulty with intimacy as an interpersonal reality. These are lonely times: Scan the self-help shelves even in a shopping-mall bookstore and you will see dozens of titles including some form of the word. The work of Robert Bellah and his associates maps in sad detail why it is and how it is that so many of us feel isolated—if not besieged—by a culture in which our own lives mean nothing at all, a culture in which we are commodities, both as consumers and as employees.[11] So when our kids fall in love, when our kids find someone "outside" to love and to be loved by, both we and they face tremendous obstacles in trying to trust that relationship enough to set boundaries to it. In a world as ruthless as ours, it takes real courage to say, "Sure I love you, but that doesn't mean . . ."

Erik Erikson suggests another dimension of the predicament we face. According to his schemata of personality development, achieving fidelity and intimacy are the primary psychosocial challenges of the teen and early adult years.[12] Kids today are facing these timeless challenges amidst an adult culture in which casual sex is commonplace and intimacy is undone by the sort of individualism that can only ask, "What's in it for me?"

An analogy may help. Do you remember learning to ride a two-wheel bike? I climbed up on the concrete incinerator behind our brownstone two-flat, slid gingerly onto the bike, wobbled forward a few feet, and crashed. I did this incessantly for two whole summers without making any progress at all. I never made it even halfway to the lilac hedge. In the spring when I was seven, I was given a smaller bike with training wheels when I made my First Communion. I rode around listing dangerously to the left, falling off anytime I tried to go around the corner. Late the next summer, when I was eight, my despairing father took off the training wheels and ran up and down the alley holding the back of the seat until I had mastered the balance I needed.

I know it doesn't take most kids three years to learn to ride a two-wheeler. If spacio-temporal orientation were as important to our culture as reading, I'd have spent my whole childhood in special ed. It was humiliating, and it was bloody. But I kept seeing all these other kids (bigger kids, at least at first) whizzing around on two-wheel bikes, so I knew that what I was trying to do was possible.

Those students I met in the late '70s didn't have that kind of confidence that sexual desire can be something more than mere appetite. Their parents were sexually faithful to one another—but parents are parents; parents are inevitably suspect. They turned to me in part, I realize now, precisely because I was *not* a parent, despite my faculty position. Not only was I not a parent, I was repeatedly mistaken for an undergraduate, even by the undergraduates. I was as close as these students could come to finding an "older kid" who clearly knew something about what they were struggling to understand for themselves.

I did have a certain confidence when Mark, our oldest, set out to master his first two-wheel bike—although I let Warren go with him. I stayed home to rummage around in the linen closet for 2 × 3 gauze pads (nonstick, these days!) and surgical tape and hydrogen peroxide. Having genetic inheritance from two very different parents, thank heavens, our three proved to be normal kids who learned as quickly as anyone does. That's not to say quickly in any absolute sense, of course. We went through several boxes of 2 × 3 pads and a couple of rolls of tape. I still keep a couple of gel-packs in the freezer. However many gray hairs I earned, I was consoled that even I had eventually learned to do this.

I was even more consoled, recently, after a conversation with a young neighbor of mine, a fabulously athletic woman whose husband is also an athlete and whose sixty-something mother is still a tennis champion, traveling widely to compete. Her two oldest kids, four and six, got two-wheel bikes this spring. She stands on her front walk, watches them wobble along, and agonizes in her memories of skinned knees. No matter what, it is painful to watch our kids struggle with new skills. No matter what, we are consoled by our confidence that, well, everybody eventually learns to ride a bike. Everybody eventually outgrows diapers too, and learns to tie shoes, and learns to say please and thank you. These are stages. They are tough, but they are stages.

Fidelity and intimacy are stages too, Erikson proposes, but as a culture we have far less confidence in anyone's success—and so it is a struggle to have as much confidence in our kids' sexual development as we might have had when they began to ride bikes. Erikson has some lovely descriptions, in strictly psychological language, of the dilemmas teenagers navigate in settling appropriate boundaries between self and other. Beyond a doubt it is complicated. But our kids need our help, and above all our kids need our confidence that this process is possible and that it is worthwhile. When the popular culture is skeptical or even contemptuous of sexual fidelity, we have even greater difficulties and therefore, I propose, a greater need for communities that pledge themselves as witness to the reality that—like riding a bike—fidelity is something humans can do, no matter how often we fall and skin our knees.

CHAPTER FOUR

The Blessing
of Sexual Fidelity

The Wager on Transcendence

Something important happens when the fullest enactment of sexual desire takes place within the fullest development of interpersonal intimacy—when physical intimacy and psychological intimacy are celebrated together in a single life-generating act. That something is what I mean by "blessing." I have been talking about blessing all along, every time I have insisted that human sexuality is not merely a physiological drive. The vitality of sex draws us into crucial relationships with each other, with prior and subsequent generations, and with all of creation. The mystery and the ecstasy and the power of sex are among the hints we have that our individual lives are rooted in a creative energy far deeper than we can fathom.

I am convinced that our lives do mean something, despite our suffering and all our uncertainties. I am convinced that we are not mere commodities and that there is more to life than earning a living. This conviction is inevitably grounded in a hope for the Holy, a hope for an energy and a creative power that transcends the grief and the greed of the world as

we know it. I'm not talking here about "organized religion."
I am wagering on transcendence, plain and simple. In saying
that sex is a blessing, I am wagering on the abiding reality of
something that I have slowly and indeed reluctantly come to
understand is far beyond what anyone can ever understand.
In saying that sex is a blessing, I am making what amounts
to a very big theological claim: Sexual union is holy, at least
potentially.[1]

No wonder we have trouble talking to our kids about sex:
The issues have a staggering depth and complexity. When we
struggle to guide our kids wisely, I am saying, we are trying
to bless their developing sexuality, to honor it as holy, and to
teach them to honor it. *To be blessed* means to belong to the
Holy, to participate in the Sacred. And in every religious and
mythopoetic tradition I have ever encountered, the key
exchange between parents and children is to be blessings to
one another. Either that, I suppose, or a curse? It is a high-
stakes struggle. For us as for them, the choices made now
will resonate for decades. For us as for them, the complex
blessing of sexuality is never easy or simple to realize. We'd
be fools to be confident. We'd be fools if we failed to look
around for help in understanding what this blessing entails,
whether we are seventeen or forty-seven.

Not Blessed but Cursed: Fidelity and Exile

I hope it is evident why "fidelity" has been such a central
concept from the very beginning of this book. Fidelity is the
norm implicit in my account of erotic desire: When lovers
turn fully and unreservedly to one another for the satisfac-
tion of their sexual desire, the bond between them can be
called "fidelity." Each turns to the other in love and in hope,

in hope of love and in love of hope, confident that hope and love are reciprocated, echoes upon echoes until the moment of climax. Each "keeps faith" with the other. There is no better word. When that faith proves to be misplaced, our most common term for what people feel is "betrayed"—the opposite of faith. Or, perhaps, "fucked." Even the mildest of people turn to metaphors like "fucked" to express their devastation at the betrayal of fidelity, because the richest sexual union, the fullest embodiment of fidelity, depends upon the union of more than reproductive organs.

"Fidelity" is also nearly a synonym for "intimacy," and it is the norm implicit in my account of intimate relationships. Intimacy arises only as fidelity is established and only to the extent that fidelity is realized. Intimacy is not possible except between people who have a profound faith in one another.

The verbal opposite of "blessing," after all, is not "sin" but "curse."[2] *To be cursed* is to be exiled, to be cut off. But I am not talking about mythic doom by a vengeful god. I'm talking about natural consequences, consequences as unimaginable in our immortal and invulnerable youth as gray hair or bifocals or arthritic shoulders. Sex is a primary energy of connection, and if we miswire its energies in fundamental ways within our lives, there begins a concealed fire whose destruction may not be evident at first.

In time, however, it becomes manifest that those who indulge their sexual desires at the expense of others have created an emotional context or a psychological domain in which they must dwell themselves—a world in which there have to be massive fortifications protecting their own most vulnerable depths from abuse. But the walls that keep them safe will also keep them separate. Erotic desire either draws us into life-giving relationships with other people or it is an imprisoning energy that condemns us—by our own actions—to the emotional equivalent of solitary confinement. Our vulnerabilities either mature into compassion or they become calloused and insensitive. Sex can be a blessing or a curse; the blessing, when it happens, is deeply rooted in fidelity between the lovers. Sexual fidelity, as I explained in Chapter One, is utterly intrinsic to everything that makes committed sexual relationships possible and everything that makes them worthwhile. That is the central truth about sex that I want my own kids to understand.

But as our own youth has subsided into middle age and mortgage payments, many of us have begun to realize that the good life is far more complex than once we would have imagined. We just don't know as much, nor as confidently, as we knew twenty or thirty years ago. For ourselves and for our kids, we are looking for "something more" in our lives than what success, social status, or material goods can supply.[3] It's a quest that began decades ago, although most of us shelved it for a while as we learned how to earn a living, how to program a VCR, how to apply for a mortgage, and so forth. But in middle age here we are again, wondering again, still wondering, how to live a life. And so, as a generational cohort, we are looking into "spirituality" in a way that the West has not seen since the twelfth century. That investigation has brought me, in the end—and despite everything that happened in the middle—to recognize that I am, beyond question, an Irish Christian.

And so, inevitably, as the woman I am and as the literary critic I was trained to be, I turn to the Bible—a potent and complicated literary masterpiece that is also the primary and inevitable source of spiritual wisdom in the West. Whether or not we are conscious of its influence or personally engaged with its spiritual depths, the Bible is as central to how we understand our lives as Chaucer or Shakespeare are to how we speak English. Despite Shakespeare's influence, however, most people find it at least initially something of an effort to read his plays. Chaucer is harder yet. Everyone needs some language study and then about six weeks' work with a Middle English glossary to begin to read Chaucer comfortably and freely. The Bible is exponentially more distant and thus more difficult than either of these poets, a fact that contemporary translations sometimes inappropriately try to disguise. Nonetheless, the Bible is the cultural locus from which arises what is distinctively Western about my allegiance to embodiment, to individual consciousness, and to actual human relationships. It is also the immediate source of the concept of "blessing."

The Bible on Blessing

There are abundant scriptural references to "blessing," column after column in any concordance. God blesses the people, and the people bless God. Individuals bless one another. Baskets and kneading-bowls are blessed, the city and the fields, our goings-out and our comings-in. Loaves and fishes, bread and wine. God dwells in the details, tradition advises us, and God's dwelling place therein is called "blessing."

Arching above or informing all of these particular blessings is the one great blessing: the loving and intimate relationship between God and humanity. Within the biblical religions, the individual spiritual journey is understood as developing from a primary intuition of what Rudolph Otto called "the idea of the Holy" into a conscious awareness of

living in a personal relationship with a God who is also—
mysteriously—a person who knows us and cares about us as
distinct and distinctively valuable individuals.[4]

We discover on this journey that establishing and developing a mature or conscious relationship with God (i.e., the
first three of the Ten Commandments) simultaneously
involves us in caring, responsible, creative relationships with
other people (i.e., the last seven of the Ten Commandments;
see Exodus 20:1–17). The parallel between the two relationships is so radical, so absolute, that it can be completely
reversed. That is, ordinarily we discover who God is and that
God cares about us by being born into a community that
knows who we are and cares about us and tells us the stories
about God and, through such actions, teaches us both to care
about others and to tell the stories in turn ourselves. Ordinarily, the child's first experience of the Holy is within that
primary psychological matrix of cared-for and caring-
about—hence the repeated biblical injunctions to tell these
stories to one's children and grandchildren forevermore. In
short, the biblical traditions regard human relationships with
an utterly central moral seriousness.

Claus Westermann has written a small but trenchant
analysis of "blessing" in Hebrew scriptures and in Christian
scriptures.[5] He argues that it is a neglected term for God's
abiding and sustaining presence within the mundane textures
of our daily lives. "Blessing" names the translucence of the
transcendent within perfectly ordinary experience. And it is
to this sustaining presence of lovers in each other's lives that I
refer in calling sexuality a blessing. Sexual fidelity is a blessing for us because it echoes in the finite this infinite blessing
that God provides.

As Westermann explains in scholarly detail, "blessing" is a
translation of the Hebrew stem "brk," an enormously rich

and ancient linguistic core whose meaning exists in something loosely equivalent to concentric circles. At its most central, the word stem "brk" refers to the awesome and mysterious "power" that is life itself. "Blessing" is the "aliveness" or the "vitality" of that which is alive, a capacity or a power that has been universally regarded as awesome and mysterious or ineffable. I read somewhere that certain Native American tribes taught their hunters and fishermen to pray in thanksgiving to the spirit of that day's catch. That's the fundamental awe and the fundamental ethical unity with all living things that the "brk" root also expresses.

Ninth-grade biology books, on the other hand, usually ask what it is to be alive and answer that question in terms of cellular processes such as the ability to absorb and convert energy. But in ancient Western thought, to be alive meant to be participating somehow or other in the Holy. Unless we continued our study of biology far into college, our vague memories of such definitions can easily reduce the concept of "life" into innumerable little pieces (ribosomes and mitochondria and histamine receptors) that seem to operate mechanically, cellular engines clattering silently along as if cells were impossibly tiny factories and we ourselves nothing more than a vast manufacturing district—Gary, Indiana, perhaps, but with dark auburn hair and green eyes. In ancient times, when we could define "life" only as "that which makes living things alive," we understood the Alive to be somehow in touch with or sustained by the Holy. Molecular biology, for all of its marvels, neither affirms nor denies that sustenance. Professional life-scientists seem to me to have at least their own generous measure of fundamental religious awe.

For the ancient Jews, the word for the sustaining touch of the Holy was "blessing." To be blessed is to be alive; to be alive is to be blessed. In its misunderstanding of both science and religion, American popular culture seems to think that there is "objective" or "scientific" evidence that our lives are random and meaninglessly mechanical events. Out of however many million sperm, this one with this set of DNA just happened to meet that particular egg, itself one of millions that just happened to develop at a particular moment. Maybe if my parents had found something better to do at that moment in June 1949, then I wouldn't be here at all. There is no "reason" that I exist, and so there is ultimately no meaning to my life. In this inappropriate and garbled popular extension of science into metaphysics, the presupposition of moral meaninglessness begins right at the beginning.

And so do the counterarguments. For the Jews and their adopted descendants, life is not a meaningless accident of dioxyribonucleic acids seeking molecular immortality. Instead, it is a blessing to be alive; life itself is a blessing. At its absolute core, at its deepest foundation, life itself is holy, and it is intimately, continuously sustained by the Holy. And that's a very different way to get up in the morning. That's a powerfully different context in which to conduct that day's goings-out and comings-in. But that's the core meaning of the stem word "brk." It is a commonplace religious belief that in our times has become a daring and countercultural claim: It is a blessing just to be alive.

The second concentric ring or layer of meaning of "brk" is "fertility." As life itself is a blessing, so also the replication of life is a blessing. Both what Westermann calls "the fecundity of person and place" and the maintenance of that fertility through health and harvest are also the core meaning of "blessing." It is, in this regard, profoundly redundant to say that sexuality is a blessing. Of course it is. In appropriate circumstances, there is no way for it to be anything else. We have a contrary heritage, of course, from the Greeks and the Manichaeans and above all from the Victorians. But the Bible itself is unequivocal on this matter from the very first pages of Genesis, where Adam and Eve are blessed and told to be fruitful and multiply—because that is what the word means or how it is that blessing first resonates within human experience.

I still remember my first kiss. I was sixteen; it was 1966. We were in the back seat of a car barreling westbound along the Eisenhower Expressway, heading back into Oak Park after a dance at St. Ignatius. The other couple in the back seat had been necking for a while already, steaming up the window on their side. I was watching with surreptitious glances. After one such glance, I found myself face to face with my date. He leaned down and briefly kissed me, then straightened up and looked out the window again.

I had no idea that such powerful feelings were possible. I wanted him to do it again, but he didn't—and I was too immobilized by my own amazement to take action myself. For years I had been sneaking downtown to see James Bond movies and the like, but none of that prepared me for this. The six of us went into someone's house for something to eat, and I remember staring at him and feeling more bewildered than I have ever felt, before or since. He never called me again, which in retrospect is hardly a surprise. Furthermore, the evening had been close to a blind date: We were acquaintances at most, not friends. That quick little kiss was hormones, pure and primal. And it was glorious. It was my very first glimpse of the erotic dimension of the life energy that is blessing.

By easy or obvious extension, "brk" also comes to be understood as success or prosperity in all of its forms: the bread that rises, the corn that raises tawny tassels to the sky, the client who signs a big contract. The winter-killed perennials that sprout from unexpected seed. Babies who transform themselves into brooding, towering adolescents when we turn our backs just for a minute. All of this is blessing, which is to say all of it is understood as God's sustaining presence among us.

Herein lies more than one sharp hook. The very first time I prepared a whole dinner by myself, something deep within me bristled at the familiar words of the grace before meals: "Bless us, oh Lord, and these thy gifts which we are about to receive . . ." Thy gifts? Nonsense! I had done all of this myself. Where was God when the potatoes boiled over, when I cut my thumb trimming carrots? Not God: *me*.

When things are going well, we want to claim credit. When we are contented in our marriages, we are tempted to say we selected our mates wisely, or we have superior interpersonal skills or great bodies or whatever. When our kids are thriving, successful, and well behaved, the credit surely is ours alone. Success easily seduces us away from fidelity to the ancient wisdom that insists that everything we enjoy, every triumph, every adept or strategic move, every fragrant summer tomato or glorious June rose—all of these things are blessings. They are not merely competence but more importantly glory, not simply achievements but more profoundly glimpses of the Sacred.

This is a crucial point and one of surprising richness as well. What does it mean to face life with a grateful heart? It is the difference, I think, between self-esteem and real serenity. No matter how competent we are, we are all of us mortal and all of us fallible. No matter how rich and how secure, we are all of us fragile and subject to misfortune. Those who face life with real gratitude live in a world of abundant beauty and generosity that is not their own work, not their own achievement, and thus—even on the darkest night—not as vulnerable to devastation as all of us discover we are, sooner or later. Sparrow tracks in shallow new snow on the driveway last night looked like stars fallen from the sky, now a deep and gleaming black, as if the echo of my footsteps in such bitter cold reverberated off the Milky Way. The smell of coffee. The comfort of these new sneakers. The noise and the energy of three kids erupting through the front door after school. Such moments are seldom more than glimmers. They are usually quick, out-of-focus flickers disrupting the quotidian consciousness that is so devoted to its own achievements. But if, as Wordsworth believed, everything that we behold is full of blessings, then the world is a good and a holy place, far, far more than our own competence and self-investment can supply.[6]

And that point reveals the second hook. How do we explain hard times? How do we cope with catastrophe, with tragedy, with infertility, with the travesties of justice and equity that parade as "policy"? When marriages dissolve into divorce, are we cursed? When the beloved betrays us, are we cursed? When our kids are remote, miserable, and in trouble, are we cursed? The short answer is *no,* because "blessing" is a profoundly complex and paradoxical reality. The long answer is the rest of this chapter, which will take a closer look at a few central biblical accounts of blessing.

After all, the Jews have never been strangers either to suffering or to spiritual paradox. The Bible records a nuanced array of arguments on this topic, arguments that we are only beginning to situate at all adequately in their original cultural contexts and literary strategies. Herein we can begin to find ancient wisdom to solace our own long, worried nights.

It was as obvious to the ancient Jews as to anyone else that "the race is not to the swift, nor the battle to the strong, neither yet bread to the wise, nor yet riches to men of understanding, nor yet favor to men of skill, but time and chance happeneth to them all" (Ecclesiastes 9:11). Nor is happy marriage a reward for virtue. The Book of Job records the good man's outrage, as do many of the Psalms. The historical books struggle over and over again with the question of whether the Promised Land is to be understood as real estate or as a spiritual state—a question that still divides Israel. Christians replicate the argument, then and now, in arguments about whether the Kingdom of God is built up by minimum-wage laws, welfare programs, laws against abortion and suicide, and so forth, or whether the Kingdom names an inner disposition roughly equivalent to what the Buddhists, generally speaking, call "enlightenment." A lot of blood has been shed in such arguments through the millennia.

For our purposes, an ancient rhetorical and didactic strategy will help to illumine the core issue. Which man is wealthy: he who has an enormous income? Or he who has everything he needs? He who has everything he needs is content with what he has, whatever that adds up to. People have been contented with very little, and people with very much have been very unhappy indeed. Which man is happy? He who has everything his heart might desire? Or he who desires no more than what he has? He who desires no more than what he has is not tormented by desires that can never be sated and by the capacity for desire that will always find some new object to covet.

Such exercises are a traditional way of explaining that blessing can be manifested as a prosperity of spirit and not simply of material goods. To be blessed can be to have the capacity to respond with creativity, grace, and serenity to whatever happens rather than to have a reliably good harvest, high profit margin, or Prince Charming in your bed. If to be blessed is merely to live happily ever after, then we would have to conclude that blessing belongs only in fairy tales. Life has never been like that—and especially not for the Jews.

But Jewish poets and sages repeatedly and delicately "redacted" or reedited their ancient heritage of stories and legends, and the fundamental literary forms of Hebrew verse and narrative are exceptionally accommodating to the slight, wry voice of visionary paradox. Consequently, "blessing" acquires a profound moral and spiritual depth without ever losing its foundation in historical, embodied, literal reality. Blessing is never "spiritualized" in any reductive way. As Jewish poets remind God—angrily and on many occasions— there will be no Chosen People left to remember God's name and to teach "all the nations" if too many more of those Assyrians descend like wolves on the fold. The community has got to survive physically and as a community. And yet, the concept of "blessing" also refuses to succumb to the escapist or romantic illusion that there is some way around the contingency and suffering of the human condition. The God of the Jews is no Mr. Fixit on high.

We can delight in what we have all the more deeply if we are not profoundly dependent upon continuing to have it. It is a blessing when our marriages work out well, and it is a deeper blessing yet to remain morally and spiritually intact when they don't: God abides among us, in short, no matter what. Confidence in that fact generates what is called "the peace beyond human understanding." There is both consoling wisdom and subversive liberation in a tradition that faces suffering so squarely and yet so boldly teaches people to pray, "Thanks be to God for what is good, bread when bread there be and the love of each other even when there be none."

When Divorce Is a Blessing

But what about divorce? What are we to think or to feel when "the love of each other" breaks down between spouses? If we are truly to envision marriage as a blessing, we must understand that divorce can be a blessing as well. We must acknowledge what common sense demonstrates: Some marriages become so destructive that the partners are far better off after divorce than they were before. But how is it possible to regard both marriage and divorce as blessings? Such paradox is slippery stuff, but it is not entirely beyond our grasp.

It is sad when people divorce for flimsy reasons; it is sadder yet when people divorce for good reasons. But the more clearly we understand what marriage involves, the less appropriate it is to suppose we can evaluate the reasons for any particular divorce. Social science investigations of divorce are good and necessary, of course; I don't dispute that. However, social scientists do not examine particular marriages but rather social and historical trends such as radical individualism that create obstacles for all marital alliances.[7] As individuals, we owe one another a generous measure of compassion when marriages collapse. My attitude toward divorce, then, is grounded upon the same insight into the character and obligations of friendship that informs my vision of marriage. Friendship at all levels is built upon generous sharing rather than skeptical evaluation. In the absence of magic wands to mend broken marriages, our friends and their children need our love. "The love of each other" abides among friends during and through divorce just as it does amidst any other tragic loss.

As Westermann's account of Hebrew etymology and Jewish religious practice demonstrates so eloquently, the blessing of all blessings is God's compassionate presence among us. That is why worship services end with a statement of blessing: In a caring community there is generated a potent energy that each person carries away when he or she leaves. Furthermore, that blessing is manifest in real and material ways by our compassion and care for one another. That is why we do not give our souls away when we are generous to one another: Blessing is a well that does not run dry.

The Ambiguity of Blessing: Abraham and Sarah

I want next to offer a quick review of a few famous biblical accounts of "blessing" so as to begin to situate our reflection within this ancient spiritual wealth and thereby, I hope, somewhat to quiet our contemporary anxiety about talking to our kids about sexual fidelity. Consider, just for a start, the covenant blessing of Abraham and Sarah.

In chapter 12 of Genesis, God tells Abraham to go to a land that God will show him. The destination is not laid out ahead of time, which is to say that Abraham and Sarah do not know where they are heading. If you don't know where you are going but you head off into the wilderness anyhow, pretty soon you will not even know where you are. In ancient times as in our central cities, such a journey could be pretty dangerous. To walk away from their own land and their own people was to take leave of everything that had secured their personal identity and assured their survival. That act sounds crazy, in the ancient world or in our own: Sane people just don't walk away from their resources and their résumés. And I think the story is meant to sound a bit crazy. I think it is meant as a poetic "definition" of the courage that fidelity entails: Everything you are, everything you have, goes on the line.

And they do not have much, by the measures of their own day. By not having children, they would have been understood as self-evidently cursed by the gods. We are to understand, then, that God shows up to a pair of middle-aged losers and proposes that they take leave of what little security they have.

And where does God send Abraham and Sarah? To a land that is still the violent crossroads of empire. Not, for instance, to Switzerland. Or Hawaii, which offers excellent isolation and far better weather. Even Ireland would have been a better choice—a remote little place where Jewish wit would have found recognition and Jewish cooking would have been a blessing to the uttermost generation. But no. The Promised Land is not a safe place, not a remote spot sheltered from most of the bloody march of history. God did not choose a couple from among the Irish, or the Swiss, or the Hawaiians. God chose Sarah and Abraham. And God's blessing left them lost, isolated, and threatened.

Blessing, it seems, is deeply ambiguous. But spiritual growth and personal change or development are always ambiguous, and they are often quite painful. It takes great courage and great faith to venture out into the unmapped land of a passionate and intimate relationship. We don't know what will come. But it will undoubtedly change us and challenge our expectations. Furthermore, each partner now has twice the liability to the slings and arrows of outrageous fortune. But the vulnerability that parents experience through the suffering of their children is even more intense than what we feel for ourselves and our partners. Surely some of the infamous tension between parents and teens originates in parents' reluctance to remember how profoundly difficult these years were in their own lives. Empathy with my own adolescents demands far more fortitude than I ever imagined.

The story of Sarah and Abraham assures us that our efforts to accept blessing are genuinely heroic. Their story comforts us when the directions of our marriages feel uncertain or the pain of ordinary misfortune diminishes our capacity for intimacy. In the marketplace analysis of marriage, as I have said before, a partnership that is not reasonably consistent in its gratifications becomes a net loss and ought therefore to be terminated. A marriage, like a business, has a bottom line. But the stories of Abraham and Sarah suggest that matrimony ought to be more wisely understood not as a transaction but as an essentially uncertain and hazardous journey toward the promise that a richer and deeper life awaits.

The legends of Abraham and Sarah also caution us that the blessings that are promised do not necessarily arrive anytime soon. These stories stand as a stern warning against the romantic silliness that leads one to expect to marry the prince or the princess and then to live happily ever after. God promises Abraham and Sarah that they will become parents of "a great nation" in whom "all the families of the earth shall be blessed." That's the opening of Genesis chapter 12, and it sure sounds great. It all gets repeated three chapters and twenty-four years later, when Abraham points out that he and Sarah still do not have a child—much less offspring numerous enough to fulfill any claim to begetting "a great nation." God repeats the promise, but Abraham falls on his face laughing. It sounds to me like the angry and skeptical laugh of an old man bitterly disappointed with his life.

God shows up a third time a year later, this time promising that *next* year they will have a son. This time it's Sarah's turn to laugh, and who can blame her? She has heard this line before. Furthermore, she is past menopause; she has known the full measure of shame and grief that would befall a childless woman in those times. The scene reminds me of a line from my Grandma Murphy: "Fool me once, shame on you; fool me twice, shame on me." Sarah is not a fool. But in a moment of potent and poignant comedy, God hears her inner laughter. Sarah tries to deny it, for she is afraid. But here is a God who can face the bitter skepticism in our hearts. When the child is born they call him Isaac, as God has instructed. The name comes from the Hebrew word for "laughter."

We can see the moral purposes of the storyteller a bit more clearly if I can tell the story again, more freely, this time translating all the Hebrew names. It might go something like this:

> Once upon a time, back in the beginning of time, the Father of All Nations and the Princess, his wife, had no children at all. But God promised them descendants; God promised that through them and their descendants all the people of the world would be blessed. So the Father of All Nations and the Princess, his wife, left all that they knew and loved and wandered the world all of their lives until they were stricken with old age. And still they had no child of their own. God made the promise again, and yet again a third time, and the Princess laughed bitterly in her heart because she knew that she was too old to give birth. But a child was born to her, and they named him Laughter, and from Laughter are we all descended.

The blessing here is not only the baby but also the vision of life that claims Laughter as one of its patriarchs. It is a very powerful little tale, rendered all the more extraordinary by how adeptly this story is woven into other stories that reflect, albeit distantly at times, actual historical memories and above all by the continuity of the worship of this God, who is still worshiped almost four thousand years later.

It is a cautionary tale as well. If sexual fidelity is a blessing like this one, if matrimony is a blessing like the blessing given to the Father of All Nations and the Princess, his wife, then we are warned that this blessing does not come cheap. As Teresa of Avila said to God some years later, if this is how God treats his friends, "then it's no wonder that your Lordship has so few!"[8] And yet we are indeed descended of Laughter, begetting and begotten in comedy, as Western literary tradition so vigorously attests. We are all born of parents who laughed at God yet remained faithful both to God and to each other until God proved that nothing is too wonderful for the Lord (Genesis 18:14a).

But then or now, sex is no joking matter. The blessed laughter here is wry and mature and close kin to pain and long-suffering: It comes late and not easily. Although there might seem to be something pious or reassuring in the thought that sexual fidelity derives from a relationship with the transcendent Holy, we need also to remember that biblical tradition describes an unfathomable and demanding God. Committed relationships—with God or with our spouses—demand everything we are and everything we have. They are a long, hard journey that is not for the faint of heart.

Sarah and Abraham caution us that the blessing of sexual fidelity is not a quid-pro-quo bargain with fate. Just as sexual desire cannot be fully developed and fully satisfied as a market-based exchange between consenting adults, so the deepest blessings of matrimony do not arrive like dividend checks from prudent, conservative investments. The Epistle to Hebrews makes the point with a beautiful image: Abraham and Sarah lived in tents, as in a foreign land, while dreaming of a city with foundations (Hebrews 11:8–10). So too, marriages are mostly lived in tents, in various drafty and temporary accommodations to shifting and difficult circumstance, and not in the brick-solid certainty we'd rather have. But a blessed marriage is a more or less wearisome and courageous process, not something made of stone set in mortar. If you spend your life mourning the solid foundation you don't have, Sarah herself might tell us, you will miss the laughter. You will not enjoy the blessings that life does provide, even if in a tent.

Or so says one of our most ancient, most important stories about blessing.

Blessing and the Struggle with Identity: Jacob

We see more of the challenge that sexual fidelity represents when we look to the blessing conferred upon Jacob on the night when he wrestled with God. As the story goes, he and God fought to a standstill, neither triumphing, until the approach of dawn required an end to the encounter (Genesis 32:24–30, as translated by Robert Alter).[9] It's a famous and very skillful story, almost entirely dependent—in classical Hebrew fashion—upon dialogue.

And Jacob was left alone, and a man wrestled with him until the break of dawn. And he saw that he had not won out against him and he touched his hip-socket and Jacob's hip-socket was wrenched as he wrestled with him. And he said, "Let me go, for dawn is breaking." And he said, "I will not let you go unless you bless me." And he said to him, "What is your name?" And he said, "Jacob." And he said, "Not Jacob shall your name hence be said, but Israel, for you have striven with God and men, and won out." And Jacob asked and said, "Tell me your name, pray." And he said, "Why should you ask my name?" and there he blessed him. And Jacob called the name of the place Peniel, meaning "I have seen God face to face and I came out alive." And the sun rose upon him as he passed Penuel and he was limping on his hip.

What did it feel like to get up limping and with a new name? Many, many of us have had nights like that, I suspect, long nights of pain and confusion so terrible that in the morning we hardly know who we are. In the early 1980s, I lost my job just months after we had bought a house with an 18.5 percent mortgage. That was a very long night, both for my husband and for me. And like Jacob, when we got up in the morning to get on with our lives, we were limping. Facing that first day took a strength and balance that we seemed not to have.

It was a long time before I realized that what felt like such a devastating loss was in fact a deep and most improbable blessing. Wandering in that particular desert, I was comforted by the ancient teaching that blessings usually arrive in such disguise. Therein, I suspect, were protected and sustained the emotional energies that made the blessing possible, that kept me open to the potential redemption of what looked so plainly like very bad news. I had not been to church in more than ten years, and it would be another seven or eight before I thought of going, but I had grown up with all the stories. Like the Irish, the Jews are a passionate and a visionary group, gloomy and witty in equal measure, prone to the telling of tales and to the aphoristic folk wisdom of lines like, " 'Tis a blessing in disguise!" It may have saved my soul.

Losing that job was painful, but it held no candle to what life inflicts on all too many people. Plenty of folks have gotten up in the morning so struck by grief that it is as if they don't know their own names. There are other biblical stories in which a person's name is changed by divine action, but afterward the new name is the only name by which the character is identified. That's not true for Jacob, who somehow retains both names, for whom past and present coexist in confusing and at times difficult ways—as is so often the case for so many of us. The metaphor of identity reflected or enacted in the question of his name is richly literary, more than we can hope to explore in this context. But consider at least this much: To what reality or what real experience might it refer when the story says his name was changed? Was there a new name on the cards in his wallet? Different monograms on his towels, a new set of luggage tags on his camels? Did everybody else know? Were notices sent out?

Obviously not. That's not how identity works, then or now, and stories about name changes are primarily stories about changed identity. Identity changes slowly. It is therefore only in retrospect that Jacob himself—or the narrative tradition preserving Jacob's whole story—could pinpoint that night at the Jabbok ford as the crucial point in his life's story and then call the event a blessing. Furthermore, the Jews take Jacob's new name as their own: They call themselves and their land "Israel." It's a bold and brilliant pun, which can be read both as "He contends with God" and "May God prevail." I can imagine no more vivid literary account of the truth that the blessing of fidelity is not a gift in a box with a gold ribbon but rather an arduous and even a confrontational process.

Blessing is no passive matter. It is a struggle, indeed a painful and life-defining struggle. The blessing follows not from victory but rather from perseverance, from the creative, generative equipoise between Jacob and God that night by the river. I am awed by the courage and the wisdom of the story, by its assertion that blessing can lurk deep within our most painful struggles with our own identity. So much blessing can come that the struggle itself might in fact be considered "wrestling with the Lord"—who does, as you recall, ask Jacob what his name is before changing it. The metaphor of naming in this story makes an incredible claim: We have to know who we are before we can set about the necessary but painful and bewildering task of growing and changing. And the ability to set about that necessary task is a blessing of the Lord, even if we fight it all the way until dawn.

Real marriages are indeed a struggle, at least now and then. A genuinely matrimonial relationship involves a lot of painful and confused wrestling around that most difficult question: Who are we? Who am I? And who are you? The Jacob story assures us that real identity emerges only from within mature and wholly engaged struggle with the central facts of our lives, from decision-making and compromise and resolute integrity forged and beaten like gold into a well-wrought art.

Paradoxically, the depth of that struggle is dependent upon the empathy of a committed, passionate, intimate relationship. Given such security, I can dare to be more than just "me." I can dare to change, to give more or to give less or to give differently than I have given before. I can dare to ask more or less or differently than I have asked before. I can dare to welcome such change from "you." The foundation of such courageous freedom, I am convinced, is built up over time from the ongoing experience of fully reciprocal intimacy embodied by fully realized sexual desire—both of which develop slowly and only within a long-term, committed relationship.

Blessing and Community: Mary of Nazareth

The stories we have seen to this point also assert and presume that blessing is never an individual matter, a private possession. The blessing conferred upon Abraham and Sarah is transmitted to their descendants, renewed in the desert of Sinai, and through Jesus Christ offered by Jews to the nations at large as adopted children of Abraham. We have often proved patricidal children, alas; but nonetheless, if sexuality is a blessing then it too necessarily shares in this public and communal dimension of the original covenant with Abraham and Sarah. My sexuality, our sexual relationship, cannot be a blessing just for me, just for us, a spiritual form of private property.

The Gospel of Luke begins with elaborately literary and parallel accounts of the miraculous conceptions of Jesus and John the Baptist. In the narrative traditions of Luke's world, miraculous births were almost commonplace, at least among certain classes of men. Such divine conception was in fact an expected feature of heroic biography—including, for instance, the emperor Caesar Augustus, who was said to be born of woman through the agency of a god. In its own historical and literary context, Luke's account of Jesus' birth is astounding not because his father was God but because his mother was a peasant.[10] The audiences of Luke's world would have been incredulous not that divinity would do such a thing but that it would happen with or to a peasant.

Luke is setting the stage not for literal-minded debates about gametes but rather for a most pointed contrast between the Kingdom of God and the empire of Rome, the way of Jesus and the way of Caesar Augustus. He does so by alluding in a rich variety of ways to previous scriptural accounts of how prophets are summoned and what famous women have sung and above all to the long scriptural tradition, going all the way back to Abraham and Sarah, of birth by divine intervention. It is a dense and very sophisticated piece of work; we do Luke a tremendous injustice if we read the story as baldly objective "fact." Luke is crafting a narrative intended to delineate a truth that journalism cannot convey. If he begins with a stunning tribute to a courageous and poetic woman, so be it. After all, Luke might easily have begun with the angel appearing to Joseph of Nazareth. That is how Matthew tells the story, and such deference to Joseph seems rather more accommodating to the prophecy that the Messiah will be descended patrilineally from Joseph's ancestor, King David. Whatever Luke's specific or personal motives for taking this narrative tack (including, of course, the possibility of otherwise unattested historical accuracy), there is ample evidence that women were prominent in the Jesus movement, in defiance of gender roles in the ancient world.[11]

Certain traditions have reduced Mary to a model of passivity, vacancy, and obedience, sometimes in accord with theories of gender privilege but more often in accord with theologies equating virtue with disembodied and radically passive obedience. Whatever its motives, that reduction ignores important features of the text. For instance, the dialogue between Mary and the angel follows the literary form used whenever someone is called to prophecy or to prophetic leadership. Furthermore, in response to this call Mary takes

considerable risks: Unwed pregnant women were publicly
stoned to death. After her encounter with the angel, Mary
departs Nazareth to stay with her aged cousin Elizabeth,
mother of John the Baptist—whose father Zechariah has
been silenced because he doubted the angel who announced
Elizabeth's pregnancy. For three months the men are silent
or absent; a scandalously pregnant girl sings to a scandalously childless wife about God's liberating and redemp-
tive power. The story is astounding. It is no wonder that
Mary has elicited such strenuous efforts at deconstruction—
or that once upon a time the nuns, the moms, and every girl
in the parish celebrated her festival in May with armfuls of
lilacs and transparently erotic energy.

The song of Mary—traditionally called the "Magnificat"—reveals the inevitably public or communal dimension
of biblical blessing, a communal dimension in which the
blessing of sexuality inevitably shares. Let's turn to the King
James version, whose poetry remains unmatched:

> And Mary said, My soul doth magnify the Lord,
> And my spirit hath rejoiced in God my Savior.
> For he hath regarded the low estate of his handmaiden:
> for behold, from henceforth all generations
> shall call me blessed.
> For he that is mighty hath done to me great things;
> and holy is his name.
> And his mercy is on them that fear him from
> generation to generation.
> He hath showed strength with his arm;
> he hath scattered the proud in the imagination
> of their hearts.
> He hath put down the mighty from their seats,
> and exalted them of low degree.

He hath filled the hungry with good things;
   and the rich he hath sent empty away.
He hath holpen his servant Israel,
   in remembrance of his mercy;
As he spake to our fathers, to Abraham and to
   his seed forever.

(Luke 1:46–55)

Notice that the poem ends with Mary's invocation of the initial covenant blessing to Abraham and Sarah, as transmitted through the generations of the people of Israel, in all their contentions and struggles both with God and with the ungodly pressures of history and circumstance. This blessing is already hers as a Jew, of course. But she claims for herself a stunning equivalence to the patriarch Abraham when she says that she will be called "blessed" by all future generations. And why is that? That's what the song explains.

At first glance, it might look as if through Mary's child God will effect a social reversal, putting down the mighty and exalting the marginalized, feeding the hungry and sending the rich empty away. But that's not how Luke's whole story ends. The story ends with the mighty still on their thrones and the poor still hungry—as indeed the world still continues these millennia later. The story ends with the ascending Jesus commissioning the disciples to preach the forgiveness of sins among all nations, beginning in Jerusalem—not outlining how to overthrow empire and distribute food stores to the starving. What's going on here? What is this blessing, or what good is it?

The "Magnificat" is neither a lie nor a mistake but an eloquent lesson in the difference between God's kingdom and Caesar's. The Kingdom of God is a visionary order, not just a set of economic principles, as the Promised Land is an inner landscape and not just arable acreage. Mary is matriarch of what Christians call the New Covenant between God and humanity just as Abraham was patriarch of the Original Covenant—both of them through offspring miraculously conceived. Her song proclaims that we are fed and exalted and blessed to the extent that we escape our slavery to Caesar and to the violence and exploitation upon which rests Caesar's reign. The power that Jesus confronts is far more than political power. It is the entrenched cultural power that tells us how to think about ourselves and how to think about others, how to construct our own prestige or "self-esteem" and how to manage our relationships and our resources to our own ends.

"To regard" something means, among other things, both to admire it or feel affection for it and to take care of it. A God who "hath regarded the low estate of his handmaiden" has thereby deconstructed the significance of status or socioeconomics or gender as the measure of anyone's worth. It's an ancient Jewish insight into the nature of the Sacred and the character of human life. Successful careers, reliable paychecks, comfortable houses in the right neighborhoods: None of these measures the human soul, Mary in effect proclaims. We need not worry about the directions of our careers, or interest rates, or even all those little lines that etch downward on our faces. And that belief is a more dangerous revolution than any army ever mounted. That belief is the most dangerous, most irrefutable challenge to the spiritual powers of darkness and oppression. That belief is why prophets and sages have always fared so poorly at the hands of the high and the mighty. Such beliefs threaten the status quo.

And so does the blessing of sexual fidelity. The blessing of sexual fidelity liberates us from the consumerist self-absorption that is the toxic heritage of radical Western individualism. Psychologists and sages alike understand that self-absorption reflects an impoverished self, that obsession with power or status reflects a pervasive terror of one's own weakness. The blessing of sexual fidelity is thus one part or instance of the ancient spiritual paradox that we find ourselves only by losing our obsessive concern with ourselves. We begin to explore the real depths of who we are only when we stop the desperate pursuit of "self-actualization." Sexual fidelity might seem, from the outside, to demand deep and painful sacrifices; in fact it is not a sacrifice at all but rather a blessing, a movement away from zero-sum cost-benefit calculations and toward the compassionate depths of generative life and the grace of that authentic prosperity that is never afraid to share.

Blessing and Rootedness: Psalm 1

History stands against the claim that prosperity rewards virtue: God "maketh his sun to rise on the evil and on the good, and sendeth rain on the just and on the unjust" (Matthew 5:45). Nor can I make a strong causal claim about the consequences of sexual exclusivity. Although the blessing of sexual fidelity requires honest and sustained effort, that doesn't mean we can earn it through sexual exclusivity any more than we can earn musical talent through earnest practice and study. Worse yet, mature and honest efforts to develop and to sustain intimacy may lead only to the discovery of ineluctable incompatibilities between spouses. Or a couple may indeed help each other to grow and to develop, only to discover that they are growing progressively further apart.

These are really unpleasant facts, but facts they are. And we need to be honest with our kids about such facts, in part because they already know plenty about divorce and in part because they are inclined toward what Paul McCartney once called "silly love songs." Starry-eyed romanticism is part of the righteous heritage of youth, it seems to me: wonderful while it lasts, painful when it ends. But a less innocently naive romanticism is also endemic to the hedonism implicit in marketplace sexual calculations. A romantic-love, happy-ever-after, just-we-two pseudomythic complex is the ideal "product" to which everyone hopes to get access.

But the blessing of sexual fidelity is not a thing or a place that you reach or fail to reach. It's not a test or a task at which you succeed or you fail. Those are the wrong categories; those oppositions are category mistakes. The blessing of sexual fidelity is a process. It is a discipline or a craft or an entire way of life. It is a spiritual practice grounded in the ultimate energies of erotic desire.

The very first song in the Book of Psalms offers a complex metaphor that illuminates how blessing operates as a spiritual practice or life discipline: rootedness. One who is blessed is rooted in a particular way; one who is not blessed is blown around or blown away by the wind. Wind is of course a very common image for sexual desire, as is another central image in this poem, that of parching heat. Note in addition the parallel verbs of walking, standing, and sitting both in the first verse and in the last two.

> Blessed is the man that walketh not in the company
>   of the ungodly,
>   nor standeth in the way of sinners,
>   nor sitteth in the seat of the scornful.
> But his delight is in the law of the Lord;
>   and in his law doth he meditate day and night.

And he shall be like a tree planted by the rivers of water
  that bringeth forth his fruit in his season;
   his leaf also shall not wither;
   and whatsoever he docth shall prosper.
The ungodly are not so:
   but are like the chaff which the wind driveth away.
Therefore the ungodly shall not stand in the judgment
  nor sinners in the congregation of the righteous.
For the Lord knoweth the way of the righteous
  but the way of the ungodly shall perish.

The poem organizes itself around a central opposition between the blessed and a cohort variously described as "ungodly," "sinners," and "the wicked." In the first two verses, this contrast is explicated through a contrast between the physical activity of the ungodly (walking, standing, sitting together passing judgment) and the interior activity of the blessed (meditation and taking delight—presented as a synonymous pair).

The contrast goes deeper yet if one takes note of the tradition whereby the law itself is understood to be utterly unchanging. It is unchanging not simply because (as the story goes) it was once literally engraved in stone but rather because the fundamental principles of just and honorable behavior (not stealing, not lying, not killing, etc.) must be timeless if they are to be valid in their grounding upon a fundamental, accurate, encompassing vision of what it is to be human. The wise understand that the application of these fundamental moral principles is no simple task, but that difficulty is why meditation on the law is so appropriate. Psalmists in particular pray repeatedly for help and instruction in understanding the law, and Jews still continue an

unbroken, ancient, acute tradition of commentary and expli-
cation. In the light of this tradition, the meditation of the
blessed contrasts all the more sharply with the busy comings
and goings of the wicked.

But the blessed is not trapped in something static or passive. The dynamic quality of blessing is elaborated in the
image of a tree, in contrast to which the wicked are but chaff
blown by the wind. The tree is deeply rooted; the chaff is
blown around. The tree is perennial, fruiting over and over
again in due season; the chaff is hulls and dry stalks of grassy
plants that have lost what fruit they once bore and now will
not bear again. Chaff is dry, by definition; the tree has leaves
that never wither.

The tree is repeatedly fruitful because it is rooted near
water, just as the blessed man is rooted in the law, which is
thereby affiliated with water—the life blood, surely, of the
parched Middle East. Chaff is without such roots, as the
wicked are without access to the life-giving sustenance of
the law. That is why (verse 5) they are incapable of standing
firm either in God's eyes or in the company of the righteous.
It's not that they are parched and blown away as punishment
for being sinful; rather, their sinfulness is what separates
them from the life-giving power of right action and the
steady, upright life.

The wind-blown image here is a poetic commonplace for
those the psalmist calls "the ungodly." Dante repeats the
image early in the *Inferno*: Outside hell itself are those who
were neither for good nor for evil but only for themselves;
they are blown around endlessly in a foul slurry of their own
excrement. Wisdom traditions variously argue, as Dante and
this psalm do, that there is no greater helplessness, no more
contemptible degradation, than to be passively subject to
one's own insurgent passions and self-centered desires. It is

the all-too-busy wicked, and not the blessed, who prove most truly passive in the end. Withered grass is an extremely common biblical image for all that is futile, ephemeral, or devastated; that's not surprising given the agriculture and the climate of the region. In this psalm, the two images combine to give us wind-blown chaff as a powerful, resonant image that defines the opposite of all that blessing entails. To be blessed is to be a fruitful tree, not straw in the wind.

The poem comes gracefully to closure in its last verse, which sets out a simple and direct contrast between the way of the wicked and the way of the blessed. The way or path of the blessed is known by God, which is to say both understood and profoundly possessed, with a hint of guardianship or protection. The way or path of the wicked, on the other hand, will "perish." It will burn itself out, blow away and be lost, come to its natural, dusty end without hope of actually getting someplace—the trail peters out in the desert within. The wicked are not punished but rather left to reach the natural end or consequence of who they are.

If we take this psalm as a guide, we can see that sexual fidelity is like a fruitful rootedness that nourishes all that we are and all that we do. It is not a single good thing that we can harvest and enjoy but rather an entire way of life that reaches deep below the surface appearances of things to sustain contact with the waters of profound and ancient wisdom about who we most truly are.

Talking to Kids About Blessing

When I claim that sexual fidelity is a blessing, I mean quite deliberately to make an assertion that I suppose some will deem controversial, perhaps outrageous. Just as sexual desire as such has to be integrated wholistically within the individual, so too sexual ethics as such have to be integrated wholistically within some understanding of what it means to be human. We cannot deal with this issue in isolation, especially if our primary concern is how to teach our kids. There is no threat—not damnation, not infection, not economic self-interest—that can hold a candle to the bonfires of youthful erotic desire. We need not threats but promises, promises of a moral and metaphysical depth that cost-benefit marketplace calculations cannot imagine, promises that radical individualism per se is apt to denounce as impossible.

The boundary condition even of erotic energy is the vision every person has—consciously or at gut level—of who they are and what that means. What does it mean to be human? As George Steiner argues, this is the "ineradicable" question of modern literature and modern life as well: Does life have a meaning, or doesn't it? Which is to say, Is there, or is there not, God?[12] One way or another, within traditions or on our own, consciously or haphazardly, we have been working that question out with our kids from the very beginning. However variously we might define "blessing" for ourselves and thus for them, we all have some understanding of some greater value by reference to which we ground our hopes—if we have such hopes—that our kids will avoid casual sexual relations.

Whatever our particular affiliations or affinities, our vision of life's deepest meanings necessarily informs any conversation we have with our kids about sexuality. But that vision is primarily and most powerfully communicated to our kids through how we live our own lives. It's up to us, for better and for worse. It's not a responsibility we can hand off to the experts, and it's not something anyone can take away.

CHAPTER FIVE

Teaching Ethics to Kids

Calling Virtue by Name

The blessing of sexual fidelity is not something we can decide to pursue or not to pursue in isolation from all the other ethical and moral concerns shaping our lives. That's a tough and complicated claim that resonates beyond the boundaries of a pragmatic book like this one. But I think it has a reasonable common-sense validity, and it is certainly consonant with Western scriptural traditions. And besides, I find the idea comforting because now I know what stories to tell my kids. I know what to say.

I suspect that most of us know, in fact. From the very beginning, most of us are teaching our kids not to lie, not to steal, not to hit. We are already teaching them to be kind, to be generous, to be responsible. We are teaching them not to exploit others and how to resist others' attempts to exploit them. Having friends and being friends is on the table as a topic almost from as early as they can talk. Even little kids quickly learn a lot about vulnerability and fidelity among friends, especially when they spend twelve-hour days either in school or in childcare programs. Grade-school play-grounds are commonly very tough places, and the loyalty manifest between children can be profound indeed.

The wisest child-rearing advice I ever read was both simple and powerful: Catch your kids behaving. Notice and comment when they do as you have asked them to do. Notice when they hang their coats on a hook rather than leaving them in a wet, snowy heap in the front hall. Notice when they start their homework without being reminded, when they put the milk back into the fridge, when they show up unbidden to carry in the groceries and put them away. All of us are quick to criticize and to complain and to prompt when their actions fall short. They need to know that we notice and care when they do things right.

I don't remember who said this. But it seemed fair and it felt wise. And in practice it felt wonderful indeed, a profound and gracious relief from the semibarbarity of life with three toddlers. I found myself almost vigilant for evidence that there was some hope, however slim, for an eventual return to civilization in my life. I needed to encourage myself, and that was about all I had in mind.

I never imagined that one day the tables might turn, that one day they would come looking for me to offer polite thanks for a clean soccer uniform, a sheet of posterboard, a box of favorite crackers. They have learned to say "thanks," and I am charmed and gratified beyond measure. Maybe they are oblivious most of the time to most of what Warren and I provide—that's inevitable and developmentally appropriate—but they do notice when anyone responds to a particular request. And they express that notice in exactly the tones Warren and I use on them.

In adolescence they are aware of us and they are aware of their friends in a whole new way because they are aware of themselves in new ways. And so they are well situated to rec-ognize that the complex integrity called "fidelity" has always been a necessary part of any real friendship. When some of their friendships begin to acquire an erotic edge—which is, for them, a tremendous discovery, no matter what they have seen at the movies—they will be blessed and strengthened by the clarity with which they understand mature relationships in general.

Furthermore, if we understand our own sexuality in flex-ible, precise ways, then we too are well situated to engage all those quick little questions about sex that kids pose when there is not much time to answer thoughtfully—en route to soccer practice or to the orthodonist. We too are blessed to know that we are talking to them about being human and about deeply intentional friendships and not just about con-traception or venereal disease. As they evolve into mature sexuality, we can help them see for themselves how this new, disconcerting experience of erotic desire reveals in a highly focused or concentrated way certain familiar truths about every friendship they have ever known. If we can under-stand, even if retrospectively, our own evolution from the ordinary friendships of childhood into the deep and mature commitment of matrimony, we can open that path of wis-dom for them as well by finding and retelling our own adventures with loyal friends and with hard times survived both by the grace of God and the help of others.

Storytelling and Virtue

Once when Warren was sick, a friend of mine stopped by with a pan of lasagna. She's a food services pro, I might add, and to call her merely a "good cook" rather understates the matter. Lasagna like hers would be worthy of Saint Joseph himself. She just rang the doorbell one afternoon and handed this gorgeous meal to the kid who went to the door and, recognizing her face, opened it.

"What's your name?" Mark asked. She paused. Her name is complicated and unusual, and he was still pretty small.

"I'm just a friend of your mom's," she said. "That's all. I think she'll know. I'll call her later."

The next day, another friend showed up with a big Ziploc bag of oatmeal cookies. She too handed the gift to Mark, who traipsed up to my study with a big grin on his face.

"Another lady came," he said, his mouth full of cookie. "That skinny one with the short hair. She said she is a friend of ours, and she just gave me all these." He fished another cookie from the depths of the bag. "This is great. How many more friends do you have?"

In our house, these stories have become legends. The lasagna lady, the oatmeal-cookie lady, and a world that was suddenly warmer and safer. Or the friend who moved to Cleveland but called someone from her former congregation to bring us a meal when one of the kids was injured. When the angel of the Lord shows up around here, it's not to wrestle or to announce miraculous conceptions but to hand over a bag of oatmeal cookies or bring in dinner. For a kid, the embodiment of care made manifest in oatmeal cookies is as real a starting place for understanding sexual ethics as any you might find.

And so, of course, is our quite inadvertent tradition of birthday cake for breakfast on the day after your birthday. That one started without any help from me: I walked into the kitchen very early one morning to find the feast almost concluded. Three faces full of chocolate crumbs, blue eyes twinkling, smiled at me and turned their cute-kid signal up to full wattage.

"Oh, Ma, you make the best cake in the world," crooned the quickest of them.

"And we had Cheerios first, honest we did," seconded another.

Oh well, I thought, and why not? Is coffee cake really any better? Or doughnuts, heaven help us? And what's disapproving worth in comparison to their waking each other up to sneak out into the kitchen for chocolate cake together at 5:30 on a Tuesday morning? Not much, I would suppose.

Stories and traditions like this are part of teaching sexual ethics too, as are any of the things we teach them about appetites or desires of any kind. If we ourselves understand how deeply all desire is one at the heart of us and how closely tied to our encounter with the Sacred, then we can face even the unruly desires and energies of our kids with something closer to peace of mind.

They did have Cheerios first, after all. And together. Surely there's blessing in such moments, a blessed hope for them and for us all.

Virtue and Tradition

But the stories we need are always more than what our own direct experience can supply. Once again, it seems, I stumbled on this fact only by falling on top of it. One day when Carol was in junior high, she told me she had rebuked two boys who were fooling around rather than working seriously on some team project for which she was the assigned leader.

"Yes, Mommy," one of them sneered at her.

"That's right!" she snapped back. "A mother is what this situation needs!"

The two troublemakers sat back and settled down to work. Carol came home more than a bit dumbfounded at herself. As she told the story I caught a glimpse in her face of a physical expression I knew all too well from my own mother. I laughed and told her she was descended from a long line of uppity women. It was, for me, just an off-the-cuff remark, a way of excusing or covering over the laughter elicited more by my own memories than by her narration. The claim wasn't so much false as concocted at the moment without due consideration of its merits.

Nonetheless, Carol latched onto my claim as if it were one of the foundational truths of the universe. Amidst the considerable guff that is an ordinary part of life for bright young adolescent girls, she holds on to that idea as once she clung to a favorite stuffed bear. When kids teased her about her willingness to dissect the frog in biology class, there it was in her soul. When kids disputed her line call in gym class or teased her about signing up for honors math, there it was again.

"Tell me another story about uppity women," she demands when she is feeling a bit unraveled. I never knew I had so many of such tales—although I have put considerable pressure on the meaning of the word "uppity."

Whether or not my claim was true when I made it, obviously I have invented what historians call a "usable past." Before my eyes I can see the claim taking shape as one of those odd facts that are constituted as true by the very act of being asserted as true, strongly filtering the familial lore about ancestral women. Do I belong to a family of strong women? I had never wondered. But now I do, by golly, retroactively if need be. I certainly have a gutsy daughter!

And here too is a lesson to be learned from our kids, at least if we start early enough. They need a useful past. They need to feel rooted in standards of behavior that support them in their conflicts with other kids, especially those who are transparently ill-socialized. When they are proud of themselves, when they know they have done well, when they know they have been honest or courageous or honorable in some way, they draw tremendous strength and resolve from the hope that these virtues are ultimately grounded not simply in their own predilections or opinions but also in the supportive power of a shared moral heritage. "Opinion" is flimsy stuff when all around you kids are cheating on tests or tormenting a helpless classmate.

Alasdair MacIntyre argues, in effect, that virtue can be transmitted in no other way. The only way anyone acquires virtues is by hearing the stories and by telling the stories that constitute a moral tradition.[1] A lifetime worth of such stories, no matter how small each one individually, cumulatively defines for our kids what we understand to be the lineaments of heroism. I use that word quite intentionally: Kids want to be heroes, both to us and to themselves. Either we define heroism, or the television does it for us. Either we name the virtues as virtues enshrined as such from time immemorial, or our kids are left prey to peers and glossy ads. Our sustained and intelligent empathy with their need to be heroes in our eyes counts for more, in the long run, than anything else possibly can.

Constructing Good Stories: Desire

When we tell a story, we create a world. It may be a small domain if it is a four-sentence tale, but there it is. Even the most complex story is still far simpler than life itself because a story has something we might call dramatic causality that "accounts for" the turns of events. The world of a story has much clearer rules, much clearer meanings, than life itself. At least at a gut level, we understand why things happen as they do in a good story. Understanding why things happen as they do in our lives is tremendously more difficult because a story is far less equivocal, far less uncertain, than a life. Stories have rules or ideas or "themes" that hold events together, that "explain why" things happen as they do. Life is not like that, except to the extent that we approach our own lives through a heritage of stories taken as reliable guides to truths that experience itself reveals only indirectly.

But in fact that is exactly how we approach our own lives. The "sacred stories" of various scriptural traditions are one instance of that. But our mundane conversational stories also embody the ethical resonance of storymaking in general, and that's a resource upon which parents can and do rely in the long, slow nurture of their children's moral sensibility. The familiar request, "Tell me about something at school today" is a request for a story, and so is, "Tell me something about work." "I remember" or "That reminds me of when" introduce stories no less inevitably as "Once upon a time." Telling stories over dinner and writing a novel are tasks of different scale and therefore differing complexity, but the inclination and the fundamental ability are apparently universal. As a literary critic per se, I am regularly astounded by the narrative complexity of the stories I hear told quite casually and informally in everyday situations by people without literary ambitions. The innate levels of the skill are very sophisticated.

We are teaching our children what they will one day need to know about erotic desire whenever we tell a story about appetite of any kind. Of course we understand that it is fun to roam around in the back of the station wagon rather than to sit wearing a proper seatbelt. Of course we understand that it is nicer to go boating without wearing a life jacket. Of course it is boring to floss teeth, or painful to get immunized, or oppressive to clean the junk out from under our beds. We all have stories about our own memories of such impatience that we can use to empathize with our kids' unhappiness. But we can also use such stories to demonstrate the key point that appetites always have to be situated within the whole of who we are. We always have to take everything that matters to us into account. Just doing what feels good in some immediate way is very seldom wise.

When I was about four years old, my family—seven of us—spent a rainy summer weekend in a two-bedroom country cottage with my aunt and uncle, a cousin, and my aunt's mother. As it happened, my aunt's mother, an extremely tiny lady, decided to improve the atmosphere that Saturday morning by cooking up a batch of glazed doughnuts. She had been a pastry chef for one of the fanciest hotels downtown, however, and the recipe in her head made a hotel-sized batch. Before long there were doughnuts cooling on every horizontal surface of the cottage—racks and racks and plates and pans and bowls of them on tables and counters, on dresser tops, in the bathtub, on the beds. It was a scene right out of Walt Disney.

Both mothers were being ordered about as sous-chefs by this diminutive dynamo, and the two dads were clearly unhappy about trying to manage six sugar-crazed kids and the incessant onslaught of yet more doughnuts. I had never had homemade glazed doughnuts before, and this grandma clearly enjoyed my awe. (I had never met such a sensible adult. I figured it probably had something to do with her size: Whatever happened to the rest of them hadn't happened to her because she just never got big enough.) Furthermore, I saw a really obvious solution to this problem of too many doughnuts.

I was in college before I ate another glazed doughnut. All of us have stories like this. Most of us probably have better ones yet, such as the first time we had too much to drink. In graduate school, I failed a set of major qualifying exams in French—but the world did not end. Nor did I, at the time, realize what a blessing the tale would come to be when my own kids were in a panic about some test. Some such stories are funny, at least in retrospect. (I certainly expected the world to end: The professor handed me my paper as if it were a roadkill skunk.) Maybe some of the stories are tragic or at least painful or frightening. Or they are embarrassing. Yet we need to understand and appreciate what a treasure these stories are. We miss the chance to use this wealth when we respond, "Because I told you so" rather than, "Let me tell you a story." The heritage of virtue depends profoundly upon the empathic telling and retelling of the stories—personal stories and, if we have them, sacred stories as well—that embody whatever we have acquired of wisdom.

Hearing Good Stories: Intimacy

In parallel fashion, we are teaching our children the foundations of morally mature sexual intimacy whenever we tell a story, however short or simple, about honorable or compassionate behavior between people. But we are also teaching narrative ethics when we listen empathically and attentively to the stories our kids tell us.

In the consumerist model of the arts, a story is something produced by one person and provided to another. But that tidy, copyrighted exchange is a reduction from the social complexity of oral storytelling practice. In real story-swapping sessions, there is a more or less richly cooperative interaction between the storyteller and the audience. A told-aloud story always emerges as a work of several hands, profoundly influenced by the responses of the audience even when these responses are not verbal. That's why some psychotherapists can be neutral listeners in highly trained and disciplined ways: It is really quite difficult and almost unnatural to stay altogether outside someone else's story. Live recordings of Garrison Keillor's storytelling transparently capture the impact of the audience upon the development of his narratives—and he has far greater and more conscious control of his material than any casually social storyteller.

This interweaving of narrator and audience is particularly evident in the storytelling exchanges between parents and children, because children forthrightly demand explicit responses. If we don't react directly, the story stops right there. I suspect that parents teach kids how to tell stories by cues embedded in our responses, cues like "So then what happened?" or "How did he react?" or "Where was the teacher during all this?" An even deeper level of teaching is grounded in every nuance of our facial expression, body language, and tone of voice. For many, many years, little-kid storytelling is nearly an emotional ballet between parent and child—a delicate art upon a parental "musculature" of tremendous strength and poise. This is an influence we cannot help but exert, no matter how deeply we respect the integrity of their experience or their need to find their own voices.

And so it behooves us to become as conscious and as responsible as we can in recognizing what deeply serious ethical issues are raised even by apparently "childish" events in children's lives. We teach the virtues in large measure by recognizing them as powerful realities that are already implicitly informing the stories our children tell: This was *kind*, that was *responsible*, something else was *loyal* or *honest* or *honorable.* That was *wrong,* that was *dishonest,* that was *greedy,* that was *rude.* We help them build narrative worlds that have a moral structure and meaning, and that's a very powerful way to help them build lives of the same sort.

No matter how confident they sound at the verbal level in the judgments they are making about "who was right" and "who was wrong," they are always looking for our affirmation. In reviewing and sharing their days, they are seeking our confidence and our help in discerning the patterns and the meanings that ought to mean the most. The deepest affirmation of all, of course, is not our opinion of what happened at school but our embodied, attentive confidence that the kid has an important story to tell and appropriate authority or judgment as its teller. What we need above all to support are the successful, daring leaps of their nascent spiritual insight and genuine moral judgment.

Tim came home one day grieving that in the last seconds of a close basketball game he had stepped out of bounds and, in frustration, launched a wild shot—that happened to go in. If he had not been out of bounds, he would have won the game. After-school sports are refereed on the honor system, and the two teams took to screaming at one another about whether or not Tim was out of bounds. He agreed with the opposing team and the argument ended there; afterward several of his own teammates lambasted him for telling the truth. Tim returned fire angrily, insisting that no game was worth lying to win. But he was at the time a small and thin little boy who was not particularly good at basketball. A winning shot would have been worth almost anything he could offer—except lying. He came home distraught.

How we respond to such stories carries more weight than any other form of moral instruction, and that is why we need to realize that the formal scope of "narrative theology" or "narrative ethics" necessarily includes the stories our kids tell us over dinner. Surely this is now a story that Tim will someday tell to any children of his own. And it is a story to which we can refer when the day comes to explain to him that sexual promiscuity is a subtle but profound variety of dishonesty. In fact, if I had figured this out for myself that day when he confronted me about condoms, I could have said, in effect, that adultery is a kind of lying. Sexual fidelity as such was not yet anything he could understand—but he certainly understood about telling lies.

Ultimately, children develop the capacity for morally mature intimacy through our capacity or our willingness to offer such intimacy to them, such due regard, such kind but firm or clear-eyed critical respect. We offer that to them in part by the quality of our responses to the stories they tell.

The Tale Beyond Us to Tell: Blessing

It is difficult to engage our children's stories and our teenagers' stories in this thoughtful, ongoing way. It is exhausting. They will talk just about incessantly to us if we listen carefully and delicately and with compassion. I know that teenagers are supposed to be monosyllabic recluses, and I suppose some of them somewhere must be, but I am finding that I was indeed wisely warned by "older" parents who cautioned me that parents are the most direct beneficiaries of adolescent introspection.

A major part of what is so tough about parenting teenagers is how immediately their stories and their concerns point out the single most difficult fact about ethical education or moral development in thc virtues. As MacIntyre demonstrates in authoritative detail, both the concept of "virtue" and any understanding of specific virtues such as sexual fidelity are essentially dependent upon a specific and prior vision of the ends or purposes of human life.[2] Implicitly and sometimes explicitly, innocent and tired parents are faced with ultimate questions about the meaning of life, questions of the sort that have occupied sages for millennia. These are metaphysical questions. These are religious and spiritual questions from which there is no escape. And there is not a teenager on earth, I suspect, who will listen attentively to parental lectures on abstract religious or philosophical issues. All we have to work with are the stories they tell us and whatever skill we have at listening creatively. Thanks be to God, I suppose, that stories are such rich resources.

The ultimate blessing of sexuality, I suspect, is how the sexual maturity of our kids coincides so acutely with all the spiritual questions raised by middle age and the sudden visibility of aging and death on our own far horizon. The pressure of this convergence can come between us like a wedge, or it can open out a whole new level of conversation, a level of interaction with our kids that will persist and grow for the rest of our lives. We don't have hard or absolute answers but rather creative hopes and ancient promises. We don't have certainty but rather an abiding fidelity to whatever traditions and communities have guided our own lives most responsibly. But we do in fact always have love. Love always abides, the greatest of these, blessing given and blessing received until the end of time.

Notes

PREFACE

1. John Keats, letter to Benjamin Bailey, 22 November 1817, *John Keats: Selected Poems and Letters,* ed. Douglas Bush (Boston: Houghton Mifflin Company, 1959), p. 257.
2. William Blake, "The Marriage of Heaven and Hell," *The Poetry and Prose of William Blake,* ed. David V. Erdman (New York: Doubleday and Company, 1970), p. 35.
3. William Shakespeare, "Let me not to the marriage of true minds," *William Shakespeare: The Complete Works,* ed. Alfred Harbage (Baltimore: Penguin Books, 1969), p. 1472.
4. William Blake, "Auguries of Innocence," *The Poetry and Prose of William Blake,* p. 481.
5. Marianne Moore, "Poetry," *The Norton Anthology of Modern Poetry,* 2nd ed., ed. Richard Ellman and Robert O'Clair (New York: W. W. Norton and Company, 1988), p. 457.

CHAPTER ONE

1. Probably the most reasonable explanation of my own spiritual orientation is to admit that I am Irish—my grandparents emigrated early in this century to the Irish ghetto on Chicago's West Side from the Gaeltachen hollows of that haunted and bloody little island beyond an island beyond the western edge of the known world. The mythopoesy of such a childhood has been described before—it is not to be underestimated. But my mature faith has been shaped far more powerfully by my study

of William Blake, William Wordsworth, and especially Samuel Taylor Coleridge. Kenneth Leech summarizes the vision that can be found both among the Irish and in these poets: "The essential difference between orthodox Christianity and the various heretical systems is that orthodoxy is rooted in paradox. Heretics, as Irenaeus saw, reject paradox in favour of a false clarity and precision. But true faith can only grow and mature if it includes the elements of paradox and creative doubt. Hence the insistence of orthodoxy that God cannot be known by the mind, but is known in the obscurity of faith, in the way of ignorance, in the darkness. Such doubt is not the enemy of faith but an essential element within it. For faith in God does not bring the false peace of answered questions and resolved paradoxes. Rather, it can be seen as a process of 'unceasing interrogation.' . . . The spirit enters into our lives and puts disturbing questions. Without such creative doubt, religion becomes hard and cruel, degenerating into the spurious security which breeds intolerance and persecution. . . . The whole of spiritual life must suffer from, and be seriously harmed by, the repression of doubt. But to the eyes of conventional religion, this mingling of faith and doubt appears as atheism. This is not a new reaction: the early Christians were called atheists." *Experiencing God: Theology as Spirituality* (1985; reprint San Francisco: Harper and Row, Publishers, 1989), p. 25.

Better yet is Emily Dickinson (*The Complete Poems of Emily Dickinson*, ed. Thomas J. Johnston [Boston: Little, Brown, and Company, 1966]):

> This World is not Conclusion.
> A Species stands beyond—
> Invisible, as Music—
> But positive, as Sound—
> It beckons, and it baffles—

Philosophy—don't know—
And through a Riddle, at the last—
Sagacity, must go—
To guess it, puzzles scholars—
To gain it, Men have borne
Contempt of Generations
And Crucifixion, shown—
Faith slips—and laughs, and rallies—
Blushes, if any see—
Plucks at a twig of Evidence—
And asks a Vane, the way—
Much Gesture, from the Pulpit—
Strong Hallelujahs roll—
Narcotics cannot still the Tooth
That nibbles at the soul—

2. In *Dirt, Greed, and Sex: Sexual Ethics in the New Testament and Their Implications for Today* (Philadelphia: Fortress Press, 1988), L. William Countryman demonstrates that New Testament statements about sexual behavior or activities reflect not the dynamics and ethics of interpersonal intimacy but rather purity codes ("dirt") and property rights ("greed"). In the ancient world, the man was regarded as the property of his family and the means whereby familial resources and identity were conserved and sustained through subsequent generations. In parallel fashion, the woman was the property of her husband, so rape was a crime not against her but against him. Any sexual activity except the production of legitimate heirs was wrong because it violated the greater economic and social needs of the extended family. In addition, the Jews observed an elaborate array of codes governing bodily fluids—not an unwise habit, as we are rediscovering—within a richly complex sociological matrix. In defiance of property codes, Jesus taught that a person cannot be regarded as a form of economic

or psychic property; he also defied purity codes as a measure of personal worth or moral status. Countryman's is a scholarly book but a very readable one.

3. There is of course an enormous scholarly literature on Jesus' social ethics, much of it highly technical, narrowly focused, and addressed exclusively to other multilingual scholars of the ancient world. One good place for everyone else to begin with Jesus as a social thinker is an astute and engaging little book by Marcus Borg: *Meeting Jesus Again for the First Time: The Historical Jesus and the Heart of Contemporary Faith* (San Francisco: HarperSanFrancisco, 1994; HarperCollins paperback edition 1995). Borg's skillful, down-to-earth account of complex issues has been honed by his teaching in a state university "in the relatively unchurched Pacific Northwest, in which the largest religious grouping is skiers followed by hikers." "The Historian, The Christian, and Jesus," *Theology Today* 52, no. 1 (April 1995): 6–16. Those who want more rather than less detail on Jesus' social program should see John Dominic Crossan, *The Historical Jesus: The Life of a Mediterranean Peasant* (San Francisco: HarperSanFrancisco, 1991). It's a very big book by an excellent writer for those who delight in long, rich reads. He briefly summarizes his principal findings as *Jesus: A Revolutionary Biography* (San Francisco: HarperSanFrancisco, 1994); it might make sense to read this one first. In a third and deeply moving book, Crossan juxtaposes early Christian art with sayings of Jesus that are probably authentic on rigorous historical grounds: *The Essential Jesus: Original Sayings and Earliest Images* (San Francisco: HarperSanFrancisco, 1994).

4. On the concept of "intrinsic" and the cultural transmission of virtue, see Alasdair MacIntyre, *After Virtue,* 2nd ed. (Notre Dame, IN: University of Notre Dame Press, 1984), especially pp. 186–196. MacIntyre's work is fascinating but very tough going in places: He writes extremely long, Germanic sentences, and he addresses a highly specialized audience of scholarly philosophers. He includes an intriguing critical history of the

concept of "virtue" and a considerable critique of individualism, however, both of which I have found invaluable.

5. Percy Bysshe Shelley, "Hymn to Mount Blanc," *Selected
Poetry and Prose of Shelley,* ed. Carlos Baker (New York: The
Modern Library, Random House, 1951), pp. 369–373.

6. On the crucial importance of community in the sustaining of
virtue, see MacIntyre, *After Virtue,* especially p. 194. On churches
as an appropriate locus for such ethically oriented, countercultural communities, see Stanley Hauerwas and William H.
Willimon, *Resident Aliens: A Provocative Christian Assess-
ment of Culture and Ministry for People Who Know That
Something Is Wrong* (Nashville, TN: Abingdon Press, 1989),
and *Where Resident Aliens Live: Exercises for Christian Practice* (Nashville, TN: Abingdon Press, 1996). Despite obvious
failures and transparent accommodations to consumerist culture, they argue, churches can and ought more widely to sustain the spiritual practices that help us resist and confront the
greed, dishonesty, violence, and exploitation permeating our
society. "The Gospel is weird," Willimon explains, "and, if you
believe the Gospel, then you will be weird. If you believe the
Gospel, you feel yourself in collision with the most widely
held and deeply affirmed values of this society. . . . Stanley and
I do believe in the peculiarity of the Gospel. Being on a university campus, I am continually amazed at how the simplest little
everyday Christian stuff is considered radical and weird"
(*Where Resident Aliens Live,* pp. 113–114). Is sexual fidelity
"simple everyday stuff"? Or am I "weird" for advocating such
a thing in our times? These two scholars are shrewd, witty,
infamously irreverent, and full of wicked questions. They have
set out to recover what once made Christianity such a dangerous threat to the international economic system and to the
Roman Empire.

7. The importance of storytelling is a commonplace in contemporary Christian thought. For a survey of its theological origins, a good place to start is *Why Narrative? Readings in*

Narrative Theology, ed. Stanley Hauerwas and L. Gregory Jones (Grand Rapids, MI: William B. Eerdmans Publishing Company, 1989). See also a fine review by George Stroup, "Theological Narrative or Narrative of Theology? A Response to 'Why Narrative?' " *Theology Today* 47, no. 4 (January 1991): 424–432. Literary folks have long recognized the moral importance of storytelling, of course. I address this confluence of spirituality and literature in my essay "Faith and Fiction: Literature as Revelation," *Anglican Theological Review* 78, no. 3 (Summer 1996): 382–403.

8. "Ode: To Autumn," *The Poems of John Keats,* ed. Jack Stillinger (Cambridge, MA: The Belknap Press of Harvard University Press, 1978), pp. 476–477. See also Hugh and Gayle Prather, *Spiritual Parenting* (New York: Three Rivers Press, 1996).

CHAPTER TWO

1. Bishop Rowan Williams, when he was Lady Margaret Professor of Divinity at Oxford, explained the extraordinary mirroring of sexual desire and explored its moral significance in a 1989 lecture printed as a small pamphlet: "The Body's Grace" (London: Lesbian and Gay Christian Ministry, 1989). Williams in turn attributes the idea to Thomas Nagel, *Mortal Questions* (Cambridge: Cambridge University Press, 1979), pp. 44–50. I am grateful to Professor Katherine Amato-von Hemert, now at the University of Kentucky, for handing me a photocopy of this lecture many years ago when we were first in conversation together about how to talk to our kids about sex. Although I draw different conclusions about the importance of committed relationships, Williams's nuanced reflection on and development of Nagel's insight has been central to my thinking on this issue ever since.

2. My opposition of "I have a body" and "I am a body" derives from Thomas McFarland's account of the psychological

stances or experiences underlying the differences between idealism and materialism. See *Coleridge and the Pantheist Tradition* (London: Oxford University Press, 1969), especially pp. 53–61.

3. "Sailing to Byzantium," *Selected Poems and Two Plays of William Butler Yeats,* ed. M. L. Rosenthal (New York: Collier Books, 1966), p. 95.

4. For Saint Paul on the resurrection of an "imperishable" and "spiritual" body, see 1 Corinthians 15:34–56. There is debate about what Paul means here, but he seems at least to be distinguishing between the Christian vision of eternal life and other, Greek beliefs that certain aspects of humankind are immaterial and therefore necessarily immortal. On the centrally important Christian idea of eternal life, see James Alison, *Raising Abel: The Recovery of the Eschatological Imagination* (New York: The Crossroad Publishing Company, 1996).

5. On the concept of heart or viscera as the single unitary source of all the contents of consciousness within wholistic spiritualities, see Thomas Taaffe, "The Education of the Heart," *Cross Currents* 45, no. 3 (Fall 1995): 380–391.

6. *The Book of Common Prayer* (New York: The Church Hymnal Corporation, 1979), p. 365. The prayer is said by the congregation just prior to the blessing of dismissal at the end of the ordinary Sunday-morning Episcopalian worship service.

7. "In man the sexual instinct does not originally serve the purposes of reproduction at all, but has as its aim the gaining of particular kinds of pleasure. It manifests itself in this way in human infancy, during which it attains its aim of getting pleasure not only from the genitals but from other parts of the body (the erotogenic zones). . . . The development of the sexual instinct then proceeds from auto-eroticism to object-love and from the autonomy of the erotogenic zones to their subordination under the primacy of the genitals, which are put at the service of reproduction." Sigmund Freud, " 'Civilized' Sexual Morality and Modern Nervous Illness," in *The Standard*

Edition of the Complete Psychological Works of Sigmund Freud, ed. James Strachey, rev. ed., vol. 9 (London: Hogarth Press, 1959), pp. 208–209. This essay is mostly concerned with the severe psychological consequences of unwilling abstinence. It is an accessible and indeed fascinating glimpse of the common human experience of life without contraception.

8. There are excellent entries on Augustine, Augustineanism, and Manichaeism in *The Encyclopedia of Philosophy,* gen. ed. Paul Edwards, 8 vol. in 4 (New York: Macmillan Publishing Co., 1967). R. S. Pine-Coffin provides an excellent short overview of Augustine's life in the introduction to his translation of Augustine's autobiography, *Confessions* (New York: Penguin Books, 1961). The massive influence and heritage of Augustine with regard to sexuality is superbly and plainly recounted in *Human Sexuality: New Directions in American Catholic Thought: A Study Commissioned by the Catholic Theological Society of America,* chair Anthony Kosnik (New York: Paulist Press, 1977), chapter 2, "Christian Tradition and Human Sexuality," pp. 33–52. If one knows how to interpret the nuances, this document is profoundly critical of the current Vatican position on sexuality.

9. *City of God,* book 14, section 16. Augustine's work is available in many translations, some of them quite Victorian in their attempts to mute or disguise references to sex. The crucial discussion is in book 14, sections 15–26. The translation I cite is by Philip Levine (Cambridge, MA: The Loeb Classical Library, Harvard University Press, 1966); see vol. 4, pp. 345–401.

10. *City of God,* book 14, sections 16, 17.

11. Ibid., sections 15, 23.

12. My friends among theologians and the clergy have doubted me on this interpretation. Here's what Augustine says: "When [in Eden] those parts of the body were not impelled by a turbulent ardor but brought into play by a voluntary exercise of the capacity as the need [for children] arose, the male seed could then be introduced into the wife's uterus without damage to

her maidenhead, even as now the menstrual flow can issue from an maiden's uterus without any such damage." Maybe there is some other way of understanding this point, but I don't see how. The 1948 translation by Marcus Dods, D.D., for The Hafner Library of the Classics follows Victorian tradition in not translating sexually explicit passages like this one: They were more uneasy with sex than even the great Augustine was.

13. John Dominic Crossan's account is characteristically adept: "Stoics sought to have as if they had not, Cynics to have not as if they had." *The Historical Jesus: Life of a Mediterranean Peasant* (San Francisco: HarperSanFrancisco, 1991), p. 75. Either way, bodily pleasure—the mere fact of embodiment—is deeply problematic: far better to be disembodied intellects.

14. Roberta Bondi distinguishes authoritatively and compassionately between such hierarchical dualisms and the wholistic visions of the very first centuries of Christian spirituality in *Memories of God: Theological Reflections on a Life* (Nashville, TN: Abingdon Press, 1995). For her too, storytelling is at the heart of Christianity as an embodied, communal practice (p. 17); she leavens her historical and theological scholarship with autobiographical musings on the consequences of growing up as a woman within Christendom's structural and ideological misogyny. She powerfully recovers the ancient heritage as a wisdom for our own times, adeptly discrediting the supposed theological warrant for the exclusion and inferiority of women. The heritage Bondi delineates was never entirely lost, as demonstrated for instance by Julian of Norwich or by the arguments about both religion and marriage among Chaucer's Canterbury pilgrims. There are strong wholistic tendencies visible throughout the Middle Ages, especially for theologians who read the Incarnation as I do (see Chapter Four, note 1).

15. *Human Sexuality: New Directions in American Catholic Thought.* On the inherent sinfulness of sex even within marriage and for procreation, see p. 42; on infertile couples, p. 39;

on the elderly, p. 41; on masturbation versus rape and incest, p. 43. Rape might simultaneously be considered a sin of violence, of course, not just a sin of lust—except that the recognition involved in that definition has come only in our times and only with great difficulty. This study offers a brief but fascinating glimpse of a millennia-long human struggle to understand our own sexuality in sufficiently nuanced ways and using the always imperfect conceptual resources of our own day. As I said in note 8, one who is sensitive to the nuances of formulations will recognize that this study is profoundly critical of the Vatican's current sexual ethic.

16. Paul R. Ehrlich and Anne H. Ehrlich, *Population, Resources, Environment: Issues in Human Ecology* (San Francisco: W. H. Freeman, 1970). They argue that problems of environmental degradation cannot be solved without first addressing the problem of excessive population.

17. Stanley Hauerwas, never one to mince words, makes this point quite clearly: "Gay men and lesbians are being made to pay the price of our society's moral incoherence not only about sex, but about most of our moral convictions. As a society, we have no general agreement about what constitutes marriage and/or what goods marriage ought to serve. We allegedly live in a monogamous culture, but in fact we are at best serially polygamous. We are confused about sex, why and with whom we have it, and about our reasons for having children. This moral confusion leads to a need for the illusion of certainty. If nothing is wrong with homosexuality, then it seems everything is up for grabs. Of course, everything is already up for grabs, but the condemnation of gays hides that fact from our lives. So the symbolic 'no' to gays becomes the necessary symbolic commitment to show we really do believe in something." *Dispatches from the Front: Theological Engagements with the Secular* (Durham, NC: Duke University Press, 1994), pp. 153–154. See also a stunning theological and psychological account of "scapegoating" translated by its author from Span-

ish into fluently American English: James Alison, *Raising Abel.* It is beyond a doubt the most persuasive argument for Christianity that I have ever read.

18. The "social marketplace" concept of matrimony is explored at length by Robert Bellah, Richard Madsen, William M. Sullivan, Ann Swidler, and Steven M. Tipton, *Habits of the Heart: Individualism and Commitment in American Life* (Berkeley, CA: University of California Press, 1985; reprint New York: Harper and Row, 1986). My critique of the trap called "individualism" is deeply informed by Bellah's work, by William Blake, by Thomas Carlyle (especially *Sartor Resartus,* London: Saunders and Otley, 1838), and by Northrop Frye, *Fearful Symmetry: A Study of William Blake* (Princeton, NJ: Princeton University Press, 1947; reprint 1969).

CHAPTER THREE

1. See, for instance, Daniel Goleman, *Emotional Intelligence* (New York: Bantam Books, 1995).

2. Andrew Sullivan brilliantly argues the political issues raised by the legal status of homosexual people. See *Virtually Normal: An Argument about Homosexuality* (New York: Alfred A. Knopf, 1995).

3. MacIntyre observes that "Although the virtues are just those qualities which tend to lead to the achievement of a certain class of goods, nonetheless unless we practice them irrespective of whether in any particular set of contingent circumstances they will produce those goods or not, we cannot possess them at all. . . . Furthermore . . . utilitarianism cannot accommodate the distinction between goods internal to and goods external to a practice." *After Virtue,* 2nd ed. (Notre Dame, IN: University of Notre Dame Press, 1984), p. 198.

4. Sir Francis Bacon, "Of Marriage and the Single Life," *Essays* (1612, 1625), *The Norton Anthology of English Literature,* 4th

ed., gen. ed. M. H. Abrams (New York: W. W. Norton and Co., 1979), vol. 1, pp. 1629–1631.

5. "For better for worse," etc., is the traditional language of Christian marriage vows, evident for instance among Episcopalians in *The Book of Common Prayer* (New York: The Church Hymnal Corporation, 1979), p. 436.

6. Matthew 6:34b.

7. I thought I was being hyperbolic, but then I learned that William Julius Wilson has in fact concocted an income-based "male marriageability index" in *The Truly Disadvantaged: The Inner City, the Underclass, and Public Policy* (Chicago: University of Chicago Press, 1987), pp. 81–90, cited in Kristin Luker, *Dubious Conceptions: The Politics of Teenage Pregnancy* (Cambridge, MA: Harvard University Press, 1996), pp. 166–169 and p. 257, n. 128. In this discussion, Luker attributes declining rates of marriage not only among poor mothers but also among even middle-class and affluent mothers both to declining real income among men and to their continued unwillingness to do an equal share of housework.

8. Jon Kabat-Zinn, *Wherever You Go There You Are: Mindfulness Meditation in Everyday Life* (New York: Hyperion, 1994), p. 248. He and his wife, Myla Kabat-Zinn, develop this insight further in *Everyday Blessings: The Inner Work of Mindful Parenting* (New York: Hyperion, 1997). Their wry appreciation of the challenge parents face is echoed by Hugh and Gayle Prather, *Spiritual Parenting* (New York: Three Rivers Press, 1996).

9. William H. Willimon, "Christian Ethics: When the Personal Is Public Is Cosmic," *Theology Today* 52, no. 3 (October 1995): 366–373.

10. John Milton, *Paradise Lost* (1674), ed. Merritt Y. Hughes (Indianapolis, IN: The Odyssey Press of Bobbs-Merrill, 1962).

11. Robert Bellah, Richard Madsen, William M. Sullivan, Ann Swidler, and Steven M. Tipton, *Habits of the Heart: Individualism and Commitment in American Life* (Berkeley, CA:

University of California Press, 1985; reprint New York: Harper and Row, 1986).

12. "The mental and emotional ability to receive and give fidelity marks the conclusion of adolescence, while adulthood begins with the ability to receive and give love and care [i.e., intimacy]. For the strength of the generations (and by this I mean a basic disposition underlying all varieties of human value systems) depends on the process by which the youths of the two sexes find their individual identities, fuse them in intimacy, love, and marriage, revitalize their respective traditions, and together create and 'bring up' the next generation." Erik Erikson, *Identity, Youth, and Crisis* (New York: W. W. Norton and Company, 1968), p. 265. Chapter 3, sections 5 and 6 (pp. 128–141), traces the process of ordinary development in adolescence and young adulthood; chapter 4, section 3 (pp. 165–178), describes behavior that is evidence of serious disruption or difficulty in this ordinary development. An earlier account situates adolescent development within a more detailed account of infancy and early childhood: See *Identity and the Life Cycle* (1959; reprint New York: W. W. Norton and Company, 1980), pp. 94–107. In the conclusion of this account, Erikson says, "I have come close to overstepping the limits (some say I have long and repeatedly overstepped them) that separate psychology from ethics. But in suggesting that parents, teachers, and doctors must learn to discuss matters of human relations and of community life if they wish to discuss their children's needs and problems, I am only insisting on a few basic psychological insights. . . . In a changing world we are trying out—we must try out—new ways. To bring up children in personal and tolerant ways, based on information and education as well as on tradition, is a very new way: it exposes parents to many additional insecurities" (p. 106). A fine Eriksonian summary of the psychology of intimacy in young adulthood is provided by Evelyn Eaton Whitehead and James A. Whitehead, *Christian Life Patterns: The Psychological Challenge and Religious Invitations of Adult Life* (1979; new

ed. New York: The Crossroad Publishing Company, 1992), chapter 3, pp. 71–88. At least in this chapter, Christianity is not in evidence at all.

CHAPTER FOUR

1. In the formal and densely abstract language of theology, the claim is this: The dynamic interaction among desire, intimacy, and blessing within an ethically mature sexual union exactly replicates within human relationships and within human consciousness the interior dynamic structure of the Sacred itself. According to fundamental and centrally important Christian theology, God is understood to have or to be a three-part interior dynamic structure referred to as the "Trinity." Sex is holy for a second doctrinal reason as well: Because of the particular dynamic triune structure of intimacy, desire, and blessing, the human act of sexual congress is a human and finite repetition of the sacred and infinite generative act of God, the essential generative activity that *is* the Trinity. The theological name for this activity is "Incarnation."

Within Christian theology at this level of abstraction, the Incarnation is not a once-and-done deal involving Jesus of Nazareth. One aspect of its manifestation began or was revealed through Jesus, but it has no beginning and no end just as God has no beginning and no end. As a result, the Incarnation is an ongoing reality within human experience. In particular, the Incarnation explains how it is that we can find energy and delight and generative joy in our own sexual unions that have their ultimate causal origins in the energy and the delight and the creative joy that is God, who made us in God's own image. This is why some Christian churches regard matrimony as a sacrament.

The claim that orgasm is potentially holy is not, therefore, at all far-fetched. There is ample indirect evidence as well. For instance, the Greek Fathers described the coinherence of the three "persons" of the Trinity with the word "perichoresis"— literally, "dancing around." The coinherence of intimacy, desire, and blessing within an appropriate sexual union is also a dance, both spiritually and in a vivid, literal, erotic, physical way. Furthermore, since the Council of Nicaea in 325 C.E., sexual generation has been an authoritative metaphor—perhaps *the* authoritative metaphor—for the relationship between the "first person" and the "second person" of the Trinity. The Christ is *begotten,* not *made* of the Father. "Sex is holy" is a substantial claim, but the evidence is strong.

2. Sin may of course be involved in sexual activity: violence, greed, lies, the abuse of power or trust, abdication of responsibility, exploitation of others. These are commonplace human wrongdoings that can be evident within sexual acts just as they are everywhere else. Our kids' sexual development merely enlarges the domain within which they are learning about the virtues and the vices. Faced with the new and bewildering energy of conscious erotic desire, they are comforted—in the root sense that includes "strengthened"—by our ability to name for them the enduring presence in this new guise of familiar moral principles we have been teaching all along.

3. Jean Grasso Fitzpatrick eloquently describes this "something more" as it appears to parents, especially to those of us who were or who have been unchurched for a very long time. It is a beautiful little book that has richly informed my sensitivity to the deeper dimensions of parenting: *Something More: Nurturing Your Child's Spiritual Growth* (New York: Viking, 1991).

4. Rudolph Otto, *The Idea of the Holy,* trans. John W. Harvey (New York: Oxford University Press, 1923). Otto was a student of what came to be called "comparative religion." He coined the word "numinous" to describe the fundamental character of religious experience as an encounter with that which is both extraordinarily daunting and yet utterly fascinating. Otto held that dogma and doctrine do not endeavor to

account for this aspect of religion; William James had already argued that such experience and not the intellectual tidiness of doctrine is at the core of religion. See William James, *The Varieties of Religious Experience,* ed. Martin E. Marty (New York: Penguin Books, 1982). Robert Coles M.D. argues at length and in several different books that children and teenagers have religious experiences no less profound than those of adults. See, in particular, *The Spiritual Life of Children* (Boston: Houghton Mifflin Company, 1990).

5. Claus Westermann, *Blessing in the Bible and the Life of the Church* (München, 1968), trans. Keith Crim (Philadelphia: Fortress Press, 1978).

6. William Wordsworth, "Lines Written a Few Miles above Tintern Abbey," *Wordsworth: Poetical Works,* ed. Thomas Hutchinson, rev. Ernest de Selincourt (London: Oxford University Press, 1936; reprint 1969), pp. 163–165.

7. Barbara Dafoe Whitehead offers an account of individualism and divorce that closely parallels my account of individualism and marriage; see *The Divorce Culture* (New York: Alfred A. Knopf, 1997). Sheila Rauch Kennedy analyzes the cruel and incoherent Roman Catholic practice of "annulling" marriages rather than admitting that they break down; see *Shattered Faith* (New York: Pantheon Books, 1997).

8. Quoted in Carol Lee Flinders, *Enduring Grace: Living Portraits of Seven Women Mystics* (San Francisco: HarperSanFrancisco, 1993), p. 174.

9. Robert Alter, *Genesis: Translation and Commentary* (New York: W. W. Norton and Co., 1996), pp. 180–183. Note 29, p. 182, discusses Jacob's change of name; note 27, p. 181, discusses his injury.

10. James Halstead, "The Orthodox Unorthodoxy of John Dominic Crossan: An Interview," *Cross Currents* 42, no. 4 (Winter 1995): 510–539, esp. 519–520. See also Crossan's *Jesus: A Revolutionary Biography* (San Francisco: HarperSanFrancisco, 1994), pp. 23–28.

11. There is now a massive literature on women's roles in the Jesus movement and in the very early church, to which useful entrance is provided by Elisabeth Schussler Fiorenza, "'You Are Not to Be Called Father': Early Christian History in a Feminist Perspective," *Cross Currents* 29, no. 3 (Fall 1979): 301–323. Fiorenza provides a longer account in *In Memory of Her: A Feminist Theological Reconstruction of Christian Origins* (1983; reprint New York: The Crossroad Publishing Company, 1992). Marcus Borg provides a brief and graceful account of the spiritual character and sociopolitical implications of Jesus' inclusivity in *Meeting Jesus Again for the First Time: The Historical Jesus and the Heart of Contemporary Faith* (1994; reprint San Francisco: HarperSanFrancisco, 1995), chapter 3, "Jesus, Compassion, and Politics," pp. 46–68.

12. George Steiner, *Real Presences* (Chicago: University of Chicago Press, 1989), p. 220.

CHAPTER FIVE

1. "Man is in his actions and practice, as well as in his fictions, essentially a story-telling animal. . . . I can only answer the question, 'What am I to do?' if I can answer the prior question 'Of what stories do I find myself a part?' We enter human society, that is, with one or more imputed characters—roles into which we have been drafted—and we have to learn what they are in order to be able to understand how others respond to us and how our responses to them are apt to be construed. It is through hearing stories . . . that children learn or mislearn both what a child is and what a parent is, what the cast of characters may be in the drama into which they have been born and what the ways of the world are. Deprive children of stories and you leave them unscripted, anxious stutterers in their actions as in their words. . . . [These facts underlie the "moral tradition" in which] the telling of stories has a key part in educating us into

the virtues. . . . I am one who can always ask others for an account, who can put others to the question. I am part of their story, as they are part of mine. The narrative of any one life is part of an interlocking set of narratives. Moreover, this asking for and giving of accounts itself plays an important part in constituting narrative. Asking you what you did and why, saying what I did and why, pondering the differences between your account of what I did and my account of what I did, and *vice versa,* these are essential constituents of all but the very simplest and barest of narratives." Alasdair MacIntyre, *After Virtue,* 2nd ed. (Notre Dame, IN: University of Notre Dame, 1984), pp. 216–218. The moral lives of parents and teenagers are an exquisitely powerful set of interlocking narratives, of contrasting—at times how sharply contrasting!—accounts of each other's behavior. MacIntyre's point is that here is nothing wrong. This is not a problem. This is what ought to be happening, however exhausted it leaves us. These arguments are the narratives and counternarratives whereby their moral sense is honed—if we listen. If we listen clearly, and if we tell our own tales with honesty and with kindness.

2. MacIntyre, *After Virtue,* pp. 186–196 and 219–225. This is a central claim in MacIntyre's dense and complex argument. His very brief, very dramatic first chapter might be read with the predicament of parents in mind.

Index

orgasm, *see* desire, erotic
original sin, 43
Otto, Rudolph, 103, 161–2*n*4

Paradise Lost (Milton), 90–3, 158*n*10
Paul, Saint, 31, 153*n*4
peer pressure, *see* community;
exploitation; friendship
Perlman, Itzhak, 18
Pine-Coffin, R. S. (ed.), 154*n*8
Plato, 24, 45–6
see also Greeks, ancient
pop psychology, *see* psychology, pop
practices and disciplines
community and, 21, 59, 87
compassion and, 76
difficulty of, 18, 20, 60, 83–4, 127
"discipline" defined, 18
embodiment and, 8, 23, 59–61
fidelity as, 8, 13, 59, 127, 128
foundation for symbolic expression,
59
as intrinsic to happiness of marriage,
13
Jewish religious, 104, 112–13
marriage as, 19, 78, 128
musical, 17–18, 20–2, 84, 127
parenting and, 10–11, 60, 69, 88–9,
133–46
spiritual, 60, 66, 69, 87, 128, 151*n*6
storytelling and, 139–142
theory versus, 10, 138–9
visual arts and, 23
see also embodiment; MacIntyre,
Alasdair; spiritual journey
Prather, Hugh and Gayle, 152*n*8, 158*n*8
pregnancy, *see* fertility
pregnancy, teenage, *see* teenagers,
pregnancy and
Presbyterians, *see* Christians
procreation, *see* fertility
promiscuity, *see* casual sex
Protestants, *see* Christians
psychology
Augustine and, 41–5
of casual conversation, 82
of casual sex 58–60
of child's experience of Holy, 103–4
of denial and projection, 84
embodiment and, 27–33
Erikson's, 96, 98, 159–60*n*12
ethics and, 45, 159*n*12

Jacob's identity and, 118–22
pop, 36, 43–6, 48–9
of psychic boundaries, 83–5
of scapegoating, 156–7*n*17
of storytelling, 142–3
of symbolic expression and
perception, 58–61
of teenagers, 54, 96–8, 134–5, 145–6,
159–60*n*12
see also repression
Puritans, *see* Christians

rebellion, *see* authority
reciprocity, 83
accepting faults, 84–5
blessing and, 103
care and responsibility, 74–7
Chaucer ("The Franklin's Tale") on,
vii
hope and love, 85, 100–1
marriage versus friendship and, 67
sexual arousal, 26, 56–8, 92, 121–2
Reformation, *see* Christians
religion, *see* Christians; Jews; spiritual
journey; tradition, moral
remarriage, 24
repression, 5, 7, 35, 36, 40–1, 44, 46, 52,
55, 56, 91, 92
see also dualism; psychology
Roman Catholic Church, *see* Christians
Rosenthal, M. L. (ed.), 153*n*3
Rubinstein, Arthur, 21

sacrament of marriage, *see* marriage,
sacrament of
self control, 32, 41, 43–4
sex education, 3–4, 9, 46–9
cost-benefit, 40–1
ethical foundations of, 40–1, 99–100,
131–2, 133–4, 146
see also casual sex
sexual intercourse, *see* desire, erotic
Shakespeare, William, vii, xii, 94, 103,
147*n*3
Shelley, Percy Bysshe, 18, 151*n*5
spiritual journey
Abraham and Sarah and, 113–18
aging and, 23
ambiguity of, 114–15
Bible and, 102, 110–11
death and, 28
defined, 103–4

erotic desire and, 24, 122, 128
helping children in, 104, 142–6,
   152*n*8, 158*n*8, 161–2*n*4
individualism versus, 66, 127
Keats on, 24, 152*n*8
Kingdom of God and, 110, 126
marriage and, 24, 68–69, 128
middle age and, 11–12, 102, 146
Promised Land and, 110
Steiner, George, 132, 163*n*12
Steinway Hall, 20–2
Stoicism, 45, 155*n*13
storytelling
   blessing and, 145–6
   challenge of hearing, 145–6
   desire, erotic and, 139–42
   fidelity and, 22–4
   intimate relationships and, 142–5
   moral issues in children's, 143–4,
      145–6
   moral resonance and, 139–40, 145–6
   sacred, 140–2
   as superior to abstractions, 23–4
   theology and, 144–5, 151–2*n*7,
      155*n*14,
   tradition and, 137–9, 163–4*n*1
Stillinger, Jack (ed.), 152*n*8
Strachey, James (ed.), 153–4*n*7
Stroup, George, 151–2*n*7
Sullivan, Andrew, 157*n*2
symbolic expression and perception, 26,
   53, 58–61
   see also embodiment; fidelity, defined;
      Incarnation; marriage, sacrament of

Taaffe, Thomas, 153*n*5
teenagers (adolescents)
   author and, xv, 12, 68–9, 145
   blessing and, 135, 142
   casual sex and, 20, 36–41, 89–93, 132
   drugs and, 36–9, 40–1
   embodiment and, 54–5, 135–7
   empathy with, 114–15
   Erikson on, 96, 98, 159–60*n*12
   erotic desire and, 11–12, 54–5, 107,
      161*n*2
   family resemblances in, 29–30, 33–4
   friendship and, 133–5, 161*n*2
   homosexual, 51
   integrity and, 60–1, 135, 144
   intimacy and, 96–8, 159–60*n*12
   parents' aging and, 11–12, 146

peer pressure upon, 89, 91–3
pregnancy and, 7, 39–40, 124,135,
   158*n*7
psychology of, 54, 62, 96–8,
   150–60*n*12 161–2*n*4
questions from, 32–3, 40–1, 55, 135,
   145–6
self-awareness and, 134–5
spirituality of, 142–6, 152*n*8, 158*n*8
   161–2*n*4
teaching, 6, 11–12, 20, 32, 46–9, 145–6
venereal diseases and, 7, 132, 135
   see also children; sex education
Ten Commandments, 13, 104
Teresa of Avila, Saint, 117, 162*n*8
theology
   arcane or inarticulate, 6, 8–9, 41, 93
   author and, xii–xiii, 9, 93, 151–2*n*7
   church community and, 86–7, 158*n*9
   Coleridgean, xii, 58–9, 93, 104,
      110–11
   grace, 85
   narrative, 24, 137, 139, 140, 144–5,
      151–2*n*7, 155*n*14, 163–4*n*1
   sex as blessing, 42–3, 99–100, 104,
      106–7, 154–5*n*12, 160–1*n*1
   ultimate grounds of sex education,
      40–1, 99–100, 131–2, 133–4, 146
   see also blessing; Incarnation;
      marriage, sacrament of;
      storytelling; tradition, moral
tradition, moral, xi–xii, 8, 12
   American Christian, 53
   blessing and, 100, 103, 111
   boundary of erotic, 132
   children's need for, 138–9
   dualist, 41–52
   early Christian, 44–6, 149–50*n*2,
      150*n*3, 153*n*4, 155*n*14
   Jewish, 103–11, 112–13, 129–30
   marriage situated within, 70
   medieval, 45–6, 155*n*14
   post-Enlightenment, 52–3
   Reformation dualist, 48–9
   sacred stories as, 139–40, 163–4*n*1
   "sex is holy" foundation for, 42–3,
      99–100, 104, 106–7, 154–5*n*12,
      160–1*n*1
   transmission of, xi–xii, 6–7, 21, 33,
      159–60*n*12, 163–4*n*1
   virtue and, 137–9
   wholistic, 31–2, 34–41

tradition, moral *(continued)*
  see also storytelling; theology
transcendence, 28, 99–104
trust, 7, 33, 38, 49, 73, 74, 80, 83, 86, 92,
    94, 96
  see also reciprocity; vulnerability

venereal disease, 13, 135
  see also AIDS
Victorians, 107, 154–5n12
virginity, 20, 43, 45, 91–3;
  see also abstinence
virtue, 133–46, 151n6, 157n3,
    159–60n12, 161n2, 163–4n1
  mysterious, 89–90
  passive obedience as, 123
  sobriety as, 37
  see also practices and disciplines;
    storytelling; tradition, moral
vulnerability, 109
  Abraham and Sarah and, 113–18
  avoiding, 101–2
  children and, 63, 67–8, 101, 114,
    133–4
  compassion and, 68–9
  difficulty of, 83, 86

erotic desire and, 26, 52, 67, 69, 76–7,
    100–1
exploitation and, 75
intimacy and, 67
maturity and, 76, 86
mutual care and, 77, 82
trust and, 73–4
  see also reciprocity

Wallace, Catherine M., 151–2n7
Westerman, Claus, 104–6, 112, 162n5
Whitehead, Barbara DaFoe, 162n7
Whitehead, Evelyn Eaton and James A.,
    150–60n12
wholism, 29–30, 54–5
  dualism versus, 30–4
  Freud and, 34–6
  hedonism as corruption of, 36–41
Williams, Bishop Rowan, 26, 152n1
Willimon, William H., 86–7, 151n6,
    158n7
Wilson, William Julius, 158n7
Wordsworth, William, 109, 147–9n1,
    162n6

Yeats, William Butler, 27, 153n3

A NOTE ABOUT THE AUTHOR

Catherine M. Wallace was born in Chicago in 1950. She received her
Ph.D. from the University of Michigan in 1977 and was Assistant Professor of English at Northwestern University from 1976 to 1982. Her
study of Samuel Taylor Coleridge's autobiography, *The Design of
BIOGRAPHIA LITERARIA*, was published in 1983. She set aside her
scholarly career in literary theory to stay home full-time with newborn
twins and a two-year-old—all three of whom are now in high school.
She has spent the past fifteen years reading eclectically, speaking and
writing about literary approaches to spiritual issues, and working as a
homemaker. Her writing has appeared in pamphlets published by Forward Movement Publications and in scholarly journals.

A NOTE ON THE TYPE

This book was set in Garamond, a typeface originally designed by
the famous Parisian type cutter Claude Garamond (ca. 1480–1561).
This version of Garamond was modeled on a 1592 specimen sheet from
the Egenolff-Berner foundry, which was produced from types thought
to have been brought to Frankfurt by Jacques Sabon (d. 1580). Claude
Garamond is one of the most famous type designers in printing history.
His distinguished romans and italics first appeared in Opera Ciceronis
in 1543–44. While delightfully unconventional in design, the Garamond
types are clear and open, yet maintain an elegance and precision of line
that mark them as French.

Composed by Stratford Publishing Services, Inc., Brattleboro, Vermont
Printed and bound by Haddon Craftsmen, Bloomsburg, Pennsylvania
Designed by Robert C. Olsson

rush mann

<enginetuning @ yahoo . com>